GUIDE
TO
GREATNESS

Other Books by Dale Christensen

Patriot's Path (2014)
– a plan for our future

Dark Horse Candidate (2014)
– autobiography

A Disciple's Journey (2014)
– spiritual perspective and religious background

Thoughts in Verse (2014)
– uplifting poetry

10 Secrets To Speaking English (2001)
– method of helping people to speak a new language

Out of Print:

The Shopping Center Acquisition Handbook (1984)
– complete process and documentation

Turning the Hearts Vol. I-IV (*1982*)
– family history from earliest ancestors to marriage

History of the Church in Peru (1991)
– selective personal and general highlights

Entrepreneur Guide: The Ultimate Business & Learning Experience (2001)
– textbook for MBA course

Teaching Improvement Program
– USTC MBA Program & Business School (2001)
– training for MBA professors

GUIDE
TO
GREATNESS

BY

Dale Christensen

Guide to Greatness

Published by:
Dale Christensen
Books@Dale2016.com

Cover design: Matt Christensen and Rachael Gibson
Editing Assistance: Jan Jackson and Susan Allen Myers

Library of Congress, Catalog-in-Publication Data

ISBN
Hardback: 978-1-942345-08-4
Softback: 978-1-942345-09-1
eBook: 978-1-942345-10-7
Audio: 978-1-942345-11-4

Printed in the United States of America
Year of first printing: 2014

"The history of the world is the biography of great people."
Library of Congress

Dedication

To every person who finds their own greatness within.

To the greatness that lies within all of us,
who can be great leaders and mentors,
who teach correct principles, inspire, and show the way
by leading and not just by telling.

Also, to the personal quest we all can pursue and achieve.

Table of Contents

Preface   1

Chapter 1: Essence of Greatness   3

Divine Attributes; Belief and Dependence on a Higher Power;
Acknowledgement of Universal Truths and Principles; Alignment
of Universal Truths and Principles; Acceptance of Every Person
as Unique and Special; Passion for Life, Liberty, and the Pursuit
of Happiness; Respectful of Experiences; Adventurous

Chapter 2: Vision Driven, Values Based & Goal Oriented   21

Mission Focused; Passionate; Goal Oriented; Self-Motivated;
Planning Habits; Time Management; Resource Management;
Good Judgment; Control Emotions; Re-energized; Values – Be
Happy

Chapter 3: Founded on Integrity   30

Honest; Word Is Bond; Reputation; Positive Energy, Enthusiasm;
Accurately Represents; Fair and Respectful

Chapter 4: Guiding Greatness   42

A Guide; Sacagawea-Guide to Lewis and Clark; Dimensions of
Greatness; Orchestra; What Individuals Do To Become Great
Leaders; Focus; Total Personal Makeover

Chapter 5: Relationship Governed   47

Establish Authority; Trust Others; Network; Alliances; Build
on Strengths; Right Person for the Job; Right Job for the
Person; Celebrate and Reward; Skilled Negotiator; Financially
Compatible; Forgive and Forget; Compliment the Team; Know
Your People; Willing to Risk; People in Others' Departments

Chapter 6: Truth Seeker   74

Teachable; Willing to Listen; Seeks Advice; Open Minded; Seeks
New Ideas; Seeks Divine Help; Alignment; Thinks Positively;
Optimistic

Chapter 7: Excellence and Quality   89

Sets Measurable Standards; Performance Focused; Results Focused; Stretch People; Obsessed with Excellence; Quality over Quantity; Definition of Success; Continuously Improve; Learn from Mistakes; Makes Adjustments; Creative; Innovative; Acts Outside the Box; Improve Ahead of Demand; Monitor Performance and Progress; Measure Performance and Progress; Analyze Performance and Progress; Focus on 20 percent

Chapter 8: Thinks Strategically   111

Strategic Approach; Anticipated Moves; Adapts to Change; Know What You Want; Know How to Get It; Alternative Plans; Exit Strategies; Does Right Things; Does Things Right; Systems Approach; Remembering People; Flexibility; Risk Taker; Risk Manager; Understands Timing

Chapter 9: Demands Accountability   123

Responsible; Life Balance; Address Poor Performance; Accountable for Responsibility; Accountable for Results; Accepts Responsibility; Strong Work Ethic

Chapter 10: Leadership Builder   140

Leader; Coach; Mentor; Vision; Ideas; Direction; Motivation; Inspiration; Decisive at Personal Risk; Involves Co-workers Present; Involves Co-workers Meetings; Develops Leaders; Understands Decision Effects

Chapter 11: Communicates Effectively   168

Brings Up Issues; Receives Input; Broad Picture; Asks Key Questions; Presents - Safe to Disagree; Seeks Feedback; Uses Feedback; Shares Information Openly; Shares Information Honestly; No Backbiting or Gossiping

Chapter 12: Service Oriented   181

Team Contributions; Benefits the Whole; Benefits Personal Interests; Helps Others Understand; Supports Others in Their Jobs; Internal Customer Service; External Customer Service; Cheerfully Does Grunt Work

Chapter 13: Resolves Conflict   194

Focus on Issues; Focus on Persons; Stays Neutral; Helps Others Stay Neutral; Not Devious; Focus on Emotion; Keeps Private Things Private; Anticipates Problems; Seeks Solutions; Accepts

Reality; Keeps Things In Perspective; One Thing at a Time;
Doesn't Give Up; Willing to Compromise; Tolerant of Others

Chapter 14: Creative, Pro-Active, and Initiative-Driven

206

Creative; Blaze New Trails; Challenge the Conventional; Search
for New Solutions; Takes the Initiative; Adapts to Changing
Needs; Sees Change as Opportunity; Sees Change as a Problem;
Learns from Mistakes and Recovers Quickly; Believes

Summary   211

Promise & Guarantee   218

Never Quit   220

About the Author   222

Bibliography   223

Preface

"Deep roots are not reached by the frost."
- J.R.R. Tolkien

Before you can truly be great you must discover and master the essence of greatness. However, the irony of it all is that most people won't be willing to discover their inner essence of greatness until they have become more familiar with greatness in dealing with others. Life is a progressive process of finding out who we really are and succeeding at whatever we can conceive.

"The ideas I stand for are not my own. I borrowed them from Socrates, I swiped them from Chesterfield, I stole them from Jesus. And if you don't like their ideas, whose ideas would you rather use?"
- Dale Carnegie.

This book contains very few original thoughts. Like good art and music, I'm not good at it, but recognize it and appreciate it when I see it or hear it. This work is an effort to take the best from the best, and help you to apply it to your own life.

Becoming great is not something one does or becomes overnight. It doesn't even happen through widely acclaimed acts of heroism or good fortune. It takes years of disciplined understanding, effort, and progress. Each of us needs to know what it is to be great, how to become great, and how to measure our progress. This book suggests some of the ideas, qualities, and processes of greatness. It also attempts to provide tools, methods, and a forum for each individual to measure, analyze, and evaluate where one is in one's own progress.

The following method of developing qualities and attributes of greatness and measuring your progress is a simple, but difficult, process. It is simple in that you have but to do it. The difficulty is in the discipline to stick with it and to measure your progress. Thomas S. Monson, said, "When performance is measured, performance improves. When performance is measured and reported, the rate of improvement accelerates!"

Read about the qualities and attributes of greatness. Give yourself marching orders to acquire them and live by them. Regularly ask yourself how you are doing. Affirm that you are progressing and record that progress. If you do this, you will realize a dramatic increase in your personal greatness which will be reflected in your stronger self-esteem and positive influence on others.

We all are unique and can be amazingly great! We can be deliberate, confident, courageous and decisive and choose wisely how to use our resources and how to spend our time. We can associate with those who recognize our greatness and walk away from those who pull us down. We can discover our personal gifts or talents and develop skills and press forward to build our character in reflection of others and on our own knowledge and experience. We can achieve greatness in our own eyes and sometimes in the eyes of others.

Chapter 1

Essence of Greatness

"The greater danger for most of us
lies not in setting our aim too high and falling short;
but in setting our aim too low,
and achieving our mark."

- Michelangelo

Hope in ourselves can be compared to a seed. If we are willing to plant the seed in our heart and let it grow, we will know that it is a good seed. We shouldn't resist by allowing our doubt or discouragement to uproot our dreams. As the seed grows and swells in our heart, we will feel it and say, "It is good." This good seed will enlighten our understanding. We will know that we have greatness in us.

Defining the Essence

Greatness is largely a matter of conscious choice. Some choose to be satisfied with good performance, or being good, rather than great. Most great people come from common, ordinary families. They see adversity as a challenge and a blessing. They are ambitious for others, not just themselves. They attribute success to factors other than themselves. When things go poorly, however, they look in the mirror and blame themselves, taking full responsibility.

3

Great people have a blend of personal humility and professional will. They often have a reserved demeanor and lack of pretense coupled with a fierce, even stoic, resolve toward life. They are willful, humble, and fearless. Their ambition is first and foremost for others, not themselves. Their concern is for others' success rather than for their own reward, riches, and personal renown. They don't talk about themselves, but deflect discussion about their own contributions. They are quiet, humble, modest, reserved, shy, gracious, mild-mannered, self-effacing, and understated. They are ordinary people quietly producing extraordinary results. They are selfless and service oriented. They never waiver, never doubt, and never second-guess.

Greatness in people evolves and occurs in extremely diverse environments, at different times and in different circumstances. Different skills are required at different stages in a person's life, and are often confused with maturity, age, and experience.

We often confuse achievement and effectiveness as the general benchmark of greatness. We lack agreed-upon measures, so it has been difficult to get agreement on who is great and who is not. We confuse greatness with individual achievement, entrepreneurial spirit, intelligence, physical characteristics, and desirable personality characteristics.

Greatness is compared more to a plow horse than a show horse. People who have achieved greatness have adhered to certain basic principles with rigor and discipline. With this dedication, they produce sustained great results. Great people evolve. They are fanatically driven and almost infected with an incurable need to produce results. Great people make a huge difference as leaders, as followers, and especially as valiant individuals.

Greatness is not defined as an absence of weakness, but rather by the presence of strengths. Greatness doesn't just happen. It comes about through conscious decisions, focused effort, and overcoming adversity.

Great people are made, not born. You are not perceived as having major weaknesses because you are always progressing and overcoming your weaknesses. You improve through self-development. No one but you can hinder your growth.

People need to be taught how to correct mistakes. Most people are more concerned about eliminating any perception of weakness than they are focused on developing strengths.

Most organizations are tapping only a fraction of the potential of the people currently in its employ. Greatness is an individual and a team effort. Everyone benefits by helping others to set even higher goals.

Great people cause the tide to rise, and lift all the boats. Everyone has talent and is a candidate for development greatness.

Possessing Multiple Strengths and Divine Attributes

"The most beautiful and profound emotion we can experience is the sensation of the mystical. It is the sower of all true science. He to whom this emotion is a stranger, who can no longer wonder and stand rapt in awe, is as good as dead. To know that what is impenetrable to us really exists, manifesting itself as the highest wisdom and the most radiant beauty, which our dull faculties can comprehend only in their primitive forms – this knowledge, this feeling, is the center of true religion."
   - Albert Einstein

5

"By coming together, singing together, reading the same words together, we overcome the isolation and solitude with which each of us ordinarily lives. We all become one and we create the moment in which God is present."
- Rabbi Harold Kushner

Great people have a belief in, and dependence on, a power greater than themselves. They understand who and what they are. They seek help in solving problems. They have strong personal values and development skills. They have interpersonal and decision making skills. They are adept at multi-tasking, overcoming adversity, and strategic thinking. They develop "Be Attitudes" including being honest, being kind, being a peacemaker, and being charitable.

Great people have humility. Humility is defined as being authentic, without pretense, not arrogant or boastful. Most leaders are very egotistical and full of themselves. What people really want from leaders are real people. Humility is not thinking less of oneself. It's about discarding false masks and being respectful of others by treating them as important people. We need each other. Arrogance and pride pretend that we don't need each other. Too often we are selective of those who will receive our attention. God created no human rubbish—only people with behavior problems.

There is a big difference between being truly great and being very powerful. An acknowledgment that "I am weak and need divine help" is the beginning of the journey to greatness. "With God all things are possible." With the right examples we can become great and lead others on correct paths. This is not religion, but a choice or quality of mind and spirit. Religion includes choices of beliefs and the practices and rituals we hold to and practice.

It requires a degree of humility to acknowledge that one is not alone and cannot succeed alone. The moment we deny such power or profess our own supremacy, we have lost greatness. When we adopt an attitude of arrogance, we erode almost all levels of greatness. At that moment, the seeds of stagnation and downfall are sown. If one develops such thinking and continues on the path, greatness turns into evil and destruction.

Acknowledge Universal Truths and Principles

Someone said, "Two diametrically opposing thoughts can both be true . . . there is no absolute truth."

However, some things are true, and others false. Some things are right and others wrong. Some things are good and others evil. A lack of absolutes can lead to mediocrity and problems. Great people teach the right way, insist on the right way, and are examples of the right way.

Many years ago, during my university years, while working as a waiter at Anthony's Pier 4 Restaurant in Boston, I overheard a group of businessmen talking very seriously over lunch. One man leaned forward in a very matter-of-fact way and said, "Look, no matter how you cut it, an apple is an apple. And that's the truth!"

His words impressed me very much, so that very day I wrote the following poem, titled *Truth Is Like an Apple*.

An apple is an apple, no matter what the way
You choose to eat or cut it, Or the price you have to pay.
It may be green and bitter, or very sweet and red.
It may be large and shiny, or withered, small, and dead.

You can carve that apple nicely or just leave it there to rot.
You can bake it in the oven, or stew it in a pot.
You can share it with a neighbor and make a real friend.
It's what you do with it that matters in the end.
Now truth is like that apple, it's very plain to see
Whether in your hand at present or in a distant tree.
So hold to the fruit of wisdom, and seek the simple truth;
For wherever it is found, the truth is still the truth.

When you don't know what you believe in, you don't know who you are. You have no idea why you're here.

We come to know by asking. Prayer and meditation, also a widely-acceptable form of spirituality, are both avenues to faith. It's an intimate conversation with your soul. Your heart knows things that your mind cannot know. A spiritual pilgrimage always brings peaks and valleys. If we wall off the valleys, we also close off the peaks.

Alignment

It is very important that one's philosophy and behavior are in alignment with the universal truths and principles that one has discovered, accepted, and lives. John Ruskin said, "What we think or what we believe is, in the end, of little consequence. The only thing of consequence is what we do."

What we do makes all the difference to ourselves and others. Someone very wise once said, "Example sheds a genial ray, which men are apt to borrow. So, first improve yourself today and then your friends tomorrow." This thought was so beautifully expanded upon by a favorite poet, Edgar A. Guest, in his poem, *Sermons We See.*

I'd rather see a sermon than hear one any day;
I'd rather one should walk with me than merely tell the way.
The eye's a better pupil and more willing than the ear,
Fine counsel is confusing, but example's always clear;
And the best of all the preachers are the men who live their creeds,
For to see good put in action, is what everybody needs.
I soon can learn to do it if you'll let me see it done;
I can watch your hands in action, but your tongue too fast may run.
And the lecture you deliver may be very wise and true,
But I'd rather get my lessons by observing what you do;
For I might misunderstand you and the high advice you give,
But there's no misunderstanding how you act and how you live.

Our greatness comes from a perfect demonstration of our example and alignment. Great people know who they are and why they are here. They act and lead from strength rather than from uncertainty. They operate from a base of fixed principles or truths rather than making up the rules as they go along. They are constant and act with correct power and practices. Those who cling to power at the expense of principle often end up doing almost anything to perpetuate their power.

Great people invite others to follow and "do what I do," rather than "do what I say." They lead by walking and working with those they serve. Don't practice long-distance leadership. True leadership cannot lift others unless we are with and serve those to be led.

Our thoughts and beliefs are paramount in relationship to who we are, what we will become, and ultimately do. Man is ultimately self-determining. Thoughts become actions, actions become habits, habits become character, and our character becomes our destiny.

Great people live in such a way that their beliefs and behavior is in alignment with universal truths and principles.

Alignment means to adjust the parts of something, in relation to one another so that they are properly positioned. Alignment means that common beliefs and concerted action are in collective pursuit of a clear result. They are in sync and coordinated. There is power in alignment. Alignment is a process, not an event. Once you gain alignment, you must constantly maintain it.

Common belief and concerted action that characterize strong alignment also generates emotions. Great leaders know how to tap these emotions and engage the hearts and minds of their team members in pursuit of results. Emotional commitment generates a deeper sense of ownership than that created by intellect alone.

Lack of alignment occurs when people remain silent and don't voice their opinion, or are inconsistent in behavior with regard to direction. When people show no visible or tangible progress they complain, make excuses, and blame others. Lack of ownership and enthusiasm causes one to disagree with a decision or direction already taken. Personal commitment and ownership lie at the heart of accountability.

Fruits of Being Great

The alignment process involves open discussion, which allows people to say what they think and be heard before decisions are made. Active participation promotes ownership and group decision-making. It is a model of council, but not of committee because people make decisions and are held accountable. Committees are not held accountable.

Alignment determines and measures personal character and capacity, which are fundamental to greatness. Character includes all aspects of healthy belief and behavior and their congruency. Capacity includes creativity, knowledge, analysis, and resolution skills. Capacity also describes a person's evolution from depending on others to independently contributing, then contributing through others into visionary leadership.

Peace and joy is a deeper phenomenon that is not based on outward circumstances. It is about inner satisfaction and the conviction of knowing that you are truly aligned with the deep and unchanging principles of life.

There is great joy in leading with authority, which is serving others by meeting their legitimate needs. This joy will sustain us on our journey through life. Serving others forces us away from ourselves and promotes growth. It all starts with a choice.

Self-Mastery

Mastery over self is the true victory. In his book, *The Seven Habits of Highly Effective People*, Stephen Covey teaches that private battles precede public victories. Self-control and the ability for self-correction is a virtue. Having a personal progress chart to identify and measure personal progress is a valuable tool.

Other keys to strengthening self-discipline include:

1. An organized workspace
2. Having the right work tools
3. Cultivating the right desire and commitment to do the necessary work
4. Just doing it!

The key is using a good planning tool, using prioritized task lists and continuous follow up with a focus on individuals.

Self-esteem is how you perceive and feel about yourself. It also includes how you think others perceive you and feel about you and how you live up to your expectations or the expectations of others. We usually measure our self-esteem by the many roles we play.

Whatever our role, we must model good behavior for others. If we are out of control, we can't expect others to be under control or behave responsibly. If you define your roles and live by your values and principles, why would you want to set a goal that is not in harmony with them?

Maxwell Maltz says in his book, *Psycho-Cybernetics*, "The 'self-image' is the key to human personality and human behavior. Change the self-image and you change the personality and the behavior."

Lewis Timberlake, in his book, *Born to Win,* says that "growth is being able to see change in yourself . . . and discovering who you are and liking what you find."

In his sales training, Phillip Russell describes success and happiness as mental habits, not goals. We are what we think we are, much like we become what we eat. If we have a good diet we will be strong and healthy, and if we suffer malnutrition we will be weak and sickly. The following statements apply to all of us: How you feel about what you do for a living has a lot to do about how you feel about yourself; How you feel about yourself determines how effective you work; How effective you work determines your success.

Behavior and Performance

There are four basic key factors that affect our behavior and performance. These key factors are:

1. Our self-image (SI);
2. Our attitude (A);
3. Our need level (NL); and
4. Our emotions (E).

Therefore our behavior is equal to $B = SI + A + NL + E$.

If we are exhibiting only A and E we are up and down. Then, when our NL's are met, our production falls. Therefore, SI is the only support for consistent behavior over the long term. It all depends on how you see yourself and how you see what you do. Coach John Wooden of UCLA was always consistent, never up and down. He created the UCLA basketball dynasty. The same applies for parents, teachers, public servants and construction workers. You too can create a dynasty in your sphere of influence. If we have a good self-image, our attitude and emotional levels will rise and our need levels will not influence us so much.

Self-talk is what you hear yourself saying as you go through the day. Are you saying happy things? Are you asking questions? Are you complaining, or being glad that you have challenges? Are you critical of yourself or others? Your self-conversation reflects an image of who you think you are, how you feel about yourself, and how you think others feel about you. Good self-esteem generates positive thoughts and actions. Poor self-esteem generates negative thoughts and actions. Be aware of your self-image. If it isn't what you think it should be, change it. You are the only one who can!

Divine Greatness in Leadership

Jesus was a listening leader. He listened without being condescending. Jesus was a patient and loving leader. He was able to level with others, to be candid and forthright with them.

It is a wise leader and a wise follower who can cope with the "reproof of life." Jesus was able to groom Peter for a very high place of responsibility in the kingdom. Jesus saw sin as wrong, but also was able to see sin as springing from deep and unmet needs on the part of the sinner. This permitted him to condemn the sin without condemning the individual. We can love those we correct. We need to be able to look deeply enough into the lives of others to see the basic causes for their failures and shortcomings.

Jesus had perspective about problems and people. He was able to calculate carefully at long range the effect and impact of his words, actions on individuals and on the whole human race. Secular leaders rush in to solve problems by seeking to stop the present pain, and thereby create even greater difficulty and pain later on. Jesus involved his disciples and gave them important and specific things to do for their development. Other leaders try to do everything themselves, which produces little growth in others. Jesus trusts his followers enough to share his work with them so they can grow. That is one of the greatest lessons of His leadership.

Jesus was not afraid to make demands of those he led. He let people know that he believed in them and in their possibilities, stretching their souls in fresh achievement. Secular leadership treats people as if they were to be coddled and cocooned forever. Jesus believed in his followers, not just for what they were, but for what they had the possibilities to become. In loving others, we can help them grow by making reasonable demands of them. Jesus gave people truths and tasks that were matched to their capacity.

Jesus taught us that we are accountable not only for our actions but also for our thoughts. Accountability is not possible, of course, without fixed principles. A great leader will remember he is accountable to God, as well as to those he leads. By demanding accountability of himself, he will be able to hold others accountable for their behavior and their performance. People tend to perform at a standard set by their leaders. They live up to their expectations.

Jesus also taught us how important it is to use our time wisely. There must be time for leisure and for contemplation and for renewal, but there must be no waste of time. How we manage time matters so very much. We can be good managers of time without being frantic. Time cannot be recycled. When a moment has gone, it is really gone. By effectively planning and taking advantage of the moment, we focus on the most vital things. We don't allow trivia or minutia to dominate or rob us of that moment. The tyranny of trivia consists of our allowing it to drive out the people and moments that really matter. Minutia holds momentous things hostage. Wise time management is really the wise management of ourselves.

To be great, we need to be selfless, not selfish; protect freedom instead of control; pursue service instead of status, and promote needs of others versus our own needs and wants. What guided Jesus's compassion, balanced by justice, versus harshness and injustice? It was his greatness.

Jesus was telling us a powerful truth about our possibilities and about our potential when he led a pathway to perfection. We are still striving and improving. Greatness is not always a matter of size or scale, but of the quality of one's life. The holy scriptures contain centuries of experience in greatness and leadership. They are the handbook of instructions for the would-be leader and seeker of greatness. To deny our destiny is to succumb to fear. To accept it and to recognize it is liberating. It opens new possibilities for life and for greatness.

Accept Every Person as Being Unique and Special

Mahatma Gandhi warned, "There will be no lasting peace on earth unless we learn not merely to tolerate, but even to respect, the other faiths as our own."

The ancient poet Rumi said, "My soul is from elsewhere, I'm sure of that, and I intend to end up there."

In Henry Wadsworth Longfellow's *Ode to Intimations of Immortality*, he eloquently expounds upon this thought:

> *Our birth is but a sleep and a forgetting:*
> *The Soul that rises with us, our life's Star,*
> *Hath had elsewhere its setting,*
> *And cometh from afar:*
> *Not in entire forgetfulness,*
> *And not in utter nakedness,*
> *But trailing clouds of glory do we come*
> *From God, who is our home.*

We rarely think of talk about where we came from or what we are here to do. Isolation of individuals is brought about by the taboo against talking about spiritual matters in the public sphere. This robs people of courage and strength of heart to do what deep down they believe is right. There has been created a moral loneliness and moral illiteracy. Absence of common language prevents people from talking about and reading about the moral issues they face.

Communities suffer from levels of crime, chemical dependence, and alienation unprecedented in civilized history. Families and children are in more trouble, and many schools are ruled by gangs and ripped by violence. Schools are under fire for closing more minds than they open. Many people hope for a heroic champion or a skilled analyst who solves pressing problems with information, programs, and policies. Both emphasize hands and heads while neglecting deeper and more enduring elements of courage, spirit, and hope.

We can enjoy all the achievements of modern civilization, yet we do not know what to do with ourselves. The world seems chaotic and confusing, and we understand less and less of the meaning of the human experience

Passion for Life, Liberty, and the Pursuit of Happiness

Most of a person's passion comes from nurturing parents. Fathers play a vital role in providing for and protecting the family. A father is the role model and example. His words and demeanor leave lifelong impressions on the souls of his children. Together the mother and father help to develop and mold the character of each child.

However, to improve the health and well-being of a family, community, or nation, the education of mothers is also vital. A mother's use of language and example in everyday interactions make her the most significant influence in a child's cognitive, emotional, and social development. Her education matters.

Parents play a vital role in educating and developing children. Both men and women, but especially mothers of the world are nurturing the rising generations. To improve the health and well-being of a family, community or nation, the education of mothers is vital. A mother's use of language and example in everyday interactions make her the most significant influence in a child's cognitive, emotional and social development. Her education matters. Mothers foster love of reading, writing, learning history, math and geography and inspire academic and personal achievement. They inspire us to be great and especially to want to care and serve.

The best investment in mankind is to nurture those who will lead the next generation. Educated woman in the home is the best place to be. The most important job is sharing values and skills with the next generation of adults. The home is the most strategic place for educated woman. Mothers foster love, values and skills of greatness and desires to care and serve.

Some argue that while advancing family life at home may be a noble cause, it does not require a college degree. They think these stay-at-home moms are misusing their education and have an obligation to stay in the workplace and shatter glass ceilings. They completely disregard the inherent worthiness of educating a human mind.

Respect Experience and Yearn for Adventure

"Great has been our past, wonderful is our present, glorious can be the future. . . . We cannot detract from their [people of the past] accomplishments. We cannot add to their glory. We can only look back with reverence, appreciation, respect, and resolution to build on what they have done. The time has come now to turn about and face the future. This is a season of a thousand opportunities. It is ours to grasp and move forward. What a wonderful time it is for each of us. . . ."

   - Gordon B. Hinckley

Without roots, plants perish. Without history, the present makes no sense. Without historical basis, vision is doomed. We honor the past. We celebrate the present by learning to do by doing. We plan and act to create our future.

The world rejects and does not understand true greatness. I applaud those who attempt to write books for the public and corporate America in a language they can understand and will accept. Nevertheless, the vital ingredients of greatness must be understood, discussed, and applied or people will only partially approach greatness and only in specific areas.

Contemporary books and articles on greatness are about aspects of leadership that the sectarian world will accept and try to understand, but the most important aspects of true greatness are being passed over, if not ignored. Many are teaching a few correct principles in a way the world will like and accept. However, the true essence of greatness is not being discussed.

We must also learn from the mistakes of others and from history in general. If we do not, we are forced to repeat them.

Give Your Best

The Olympic motto, "Stronger, Higher, Faster" is the hope and driving force for many. It is being seen and felt more and more by people all over the earth. To just know that it is possible is enough to inspire the mind and heart to new and better possibilities.

The Olympic athletes see the vision, they dream the dream, and then they relentlessly and courageously pursue their goals. Most of them risk everything, including their health and safety, to not only win the gold medal, but to just participate and compete as an Olympic athlete in the world games. They invest their time, energy, money and future in an effort to achieve their goal.

Greatness is founded on true principles and practices. It was created by people willing to risk all to achieve something new and better for themselves and especially for their posterity. There are always some who perpetuate this motto and there are always others who cling to the status quo or even try to discredit it.

Chapter 2

Vision Driven, Values Based
and Goal Oriented

"Where there is no vision the people perish."
- Proverbs 29:18

Conversely, where there *is* vision the people flourish! Greatness seeks vision, captures vision, shares vision, and inspires vision.

A Personal Mission Statement

Your vision will be defined and stated in your personal mission statement. Keep in mind that in your mission statement, values and goals should be written in the form of an affirmation, which is a "A positive factual statement of a desired status or result that is stated as though it is already complete or realized." This is an example of seeking, capturing, sharing, and inspiring vision.

Just as with a company mission statement, your personal mission statement is one of the most powerful and significant things you can do for yourself and your family. It will help you to define your values and goals. It will describe who you are and what you want to be. It will also determine what contributions you want to make to society and what you want to be known for and remembered for. All the values, goals, daily tasks, and the decisions you will make in the future will be based upon your personal mission statement. It will be your beacon light or compass and a source of guidance for you amid the stormy seas and pressing, pulling currents of life. Great people keep clearly focused on their mission and purpose. Examples of mission statements could be:

1. We make the best bagels in the world;
2. I am my customer's servant;
3. We are always faithful; or
4. I deliver energy.

Values Based

Your personal or life values are unique to you and reflect the things that matter most to you. Values equal your highest priorities. Your values may include family, happiness, health, wealth, honesty, education, intelligence, creativity, etc. The values are stated as affirmations and describe what you value the most in life. Great people know and preserve their purpose and core values and establish goals based on their purpose and these values. Their strategies and operating practices will adapt to a changing world. Some examples of values might be: 1) I am physically fit; 2) I am financially independent; 3) I am environmentally aware; or I am a wise steward.

Goal Oriented and Self-Motivated

"Without a goal, there can be no real success . . . the trouble with not having a goal is that you can spend your life running up and down the field and never crossing the goal line."
    - Thomas S. Monson

With a clear mission statement and defined values in place, we are ready to establish goals of who we want to be, what we want to accomplish or where we want to go. Other goals will help us know how to do this and when. First, we must think in terms of *results* in order to establish meaningful goals. Getting feedback from others will help us understand why change in our personal life or in an organization is needed. As an individual or in a group or organization, claiming accountability for current and past results creates a powerful and positive experience. Blaming others for our problems, situation or choices will not help us to progress. If we accept responsibility for our decisions and future, we are prepared to succeed.

Even in groups and large organizations, we must accept personal responsibility for our individual success and for the success of our team. Don't allow different functions or "silos" to divide you. Maintain the attitude that nobody wins unless everyone wins. Everyone holds everyone accountable for all results. Goals are powerful! Individually and as a group, we need to understand how to set goals and how to use them to our advantage.

Personal Preparation

It is reported that 95 percent of people who reach age 65 years are on some kind of support, and only 5 percent are financially independent. The main reason for this is lack of effective goals. "Be Prepared", is the motto of the Boy Scouts of America and is good for everyone. You need a foundation of knowledge upon which to base your actions. There is no substitute for preparation. Give it the necessary time and attention. Inadequate preparation produces inadequate results.

Long-range goals focus on our destination, or horizon. Intermediate goals help us move from where we are to the next step. Daily goals or tasks are incremental steps that we do today to move toward the intermediate long range goals.

"We do believe in setting goals. We live by goals. In athletics we always have a goal. When we go to school, we have the goal of graduation and degrees. Our total existence is goal-oriented. We must have goals to make progress, encouraged by keeping records. I believe it is proper for a [person] to set his own goals, as the swimmer or the jumper or the runner does. Goals are good. Laboring with a distant aim sets the mind in a higher key and puts us at our best."
- Spencer W. Kimball

SMART Goals

Goals have the following characteristics in order to be effective:

S = Specific and focused on activity and results
M = Measurable and defined
A = Achievable
R = Realistic
T = Time dimensioned with dateTt

Examples of a goal that meets these criteria could be:

1. Save $10,000 in gold coins by December 31, 2020;
2. Run the Boston Marathon in 2019;
3. Pay off my student loans by June 30, 2017; or
4. Read the Bible from cover to cover over the next twelve months.

Goal, Objective, and Strategy

To better understand the process of setting goals, let's talk about some basic terms we all use, but we sometimes use very differently. We are all familiar with terms such as goal, objective, and strategy.

- The *Goal* is a desired result that answers the questions: What? When? How much?
- The *Objective* is the purpose for achieving the desired result and which answers the question: W*hy*?
- *Strategy* is the method of achieving the results and answers the question: How?

Goals, objectives, and strategies should focus on both *activities* and *results*. They always involve ideals and effort. They describe the future so it can become a reality in the present.

An example of explain your goals in terms of objectives and strategies could be:

- I will complete the Boston Marathon (goal)
- so I can stay in shape and loose twenty pounds (objective)
- by running 5 miles 4 days a week and 10 miles 2 days a week for the next six months (strategy).

As you can see, these are expressed in both activities and results.

Planning habits

An old Chinese proverb warns, "If you do not change your direction, you will end up exactly where you are headed." Planning is the process of pre-determining the course of thoughts, expected emotions, actions, and events in order to achieve desired results. Planning is like preventive maintenance which will help avoid mistakes, stay on course, and adjust when needed.

A plan puts you in charge of your energies and activities. Have a plan and adhere to it unfailingly. Know where you are going, and go there. Don't let anything deter you. Be resolute carry out your plan.

Master the art of following the specific steps to effective planning:

1. Review highest priorities and goals
2. Identify specific events, thoughts, or actions
3. Compare time required for each
4. Evaluate resources and opposition
5. Prioritize each against the other

There are always excuses for not planning. They include these often-heard statements:

- Planning limits freedom;
- I am operating under crisis management right now;
- I have no time to plan.

Do not accept or give in to these ideas, and avoid them at all costs.

Prioritization

"The tyranny of the urgent: Urgency engulfs the (life/time) manager; yet the most urgent task is not always the most important. The tyranny of the urgent lies in its distortion of priorities. . . .

One of the measures of a manager is [the] ability to distinguish the important from the urgent, to refuse to be tyrannized by the urgent, to refuse to manage by crisis."
  - R. Alex Mackenzie, *The Time Trap*

Be focused and stay focused. Usually, setting priorities is not a problem. The problem comes in getting distracted from them, going off on tangents, and letting "good" things crowd out the "best" things. The priorities of our lives don't have to be incompatible with priorities for success. Prioritization is the giving value and order to the thoughts, actions, and events.

Consider the *80/20 Rule* which states that 80 percent of the positive results come from 20 percent of the effort. Likewise, 80 percent of the knowledge is found in 20 percent of the text, notes, or lecture material, etc. 80 percent of your success will come from 20 percent of the market or business efforts. The key is to identify that 20 percent and focus your efforts on it. First identify all the goals and tasks relating to this 20 percent. Once the goals and tasks are identified and written down, they need to be prioritized.

Prioritization is the giving of value and order to thoughts, actions, and events. We can make things happen by prioritizing tasks. First, make a daily task list. Then give them a value of A = vital; B = important; and C = nice to do. Further prioritize them by giving them a number, such as A1, A2, A3, and B1, B2, and C1, C2, etc.

A priority list would look something like the following:

A1   Attend John and Mary's wedding
A2   Get my tax report in by April 10th
A3   Attend Billy's soccer match

B1   Call Frank about the Meltzer account
B2   Have the pickup's engine tuned up and oil changes
C1   Watch Monday night football Rick
C2   Pick up the laundry

Managing Time and Resources

"A lot of people spend much of their time filling their life with time. I hope you'll fill your time with life."
- Ellen Silverberg Brannen

"To everything there is a season, and a time to every purpose under the heaven. . . ."
- Ecclesiastes 3:1

"Every day, every hour, every minute of your span of mortal years must sometime be accounted for. And it is in this life that you walk by faith and prove yourself able to choose good over evil, right over wrong, enduring happiness over mere amusement. And your eternal reward will be according to your choosing."
- Richard L. Evans

"Time stays long enough for those who use it."
- Leonardo Da Vinci

"Dost thou love life? Then do not squander time, for that's the stuff life is made of."
- Benjamin Franklin

"Hours and days, months and years, pass away, and time once past never returns."
- Cicero

Personal Productivity Plan

Greatness begins with planning and work. Your personal productivity plan will include:

1. Your personal mission statement of who you want to be
2. Your personal idea of what is of most value to you
3. Your long-range, intermediate, and short-term goals
4. A way to manager your daily tasks to achieve those goals, live your values, and realize your mission statement.

To do this you will need an on-line program or day planner. You should have a place to write task lists, a calendar for appointments, and a place to record important events and information. Your planner (paper or electronic) can be carried in your pocket, purse or briefcase. There are many great tools to choose from – so choose one and use it!

Chapter 3

Founded on Integrity

". . . till I die I will not remove mine integrity from me."
- Job 27:5

Honesty is being free from deception. To be great, you must be totally honest, and guard your integrity and reputation. Commitment is sticking to your choices. Help develop cultures that honestly confront brutal facts and difficult challenges. Make your word your bond and consider your reputation sacred.

There may be situations where you may need to compromise. It is appropriate to compromise on process, but never on principle. We should always be willing to listen to the opinions of others and cultivate an open mind and a flexible approach to problem solving. And yet, there are also times when we need to take a stand, define our position, and refuse to back down. Such moments may be fairly rare, but those moments which most define us are those where we are forced to choose, once and for all, where we stand.

For Sir Thomas Moore, such a defining moment came when he was asked to take an oath that violated everything he believed in. By refusing to take such an oath, Moore was imprisoned, his lands confiscated, his life placed in peril. Yet when asked by his daughter to free himself and simply take the oath, his reply speaks to us all, "When a man takes an oath, he holds himself in his own hands. Like water. And if he opens his fingers again, he needn't hope to find himself again." Moore's stalwart refusal to violate his own sense of self by taking a false oath led to his execution, but left us a great legacy of courage and integrity.

Perhaps we'll define our own integrity in matters of small proportion – in a decision not to run a red a light at an intersection or a decision to return extra change given us by a store clerk. It may be expressed in a promise made to a child or a commitment made to a neighbor. These are all a kind of oath.

People are dishonest because they want to quickly gain the advantage they haven't spent the time to earn. Dishonesty may gain the advantage for the moment, but will leave us empty handed in the long run. Benefits of honesty include peace of mind, satisfaction, inner strength, and confidence. We develop trust, influence, and self-respect. We have nothing to hide and can look anyone in the eye. Have the moral courage to make your actions consistent with your knowledge of right and wrong.

Queen Esther

Ester was the Queen of Persia in the *Old Testament*. She was a woman of pure integrity and love for her people. The Jews were in grave danger of being destroyed and she was the only one who could intercede for them with the King. Esther had the courage to stand for truth and righteousness although it meant placing her life in grave danger, as she literally offered it up to save her people from execution.

Take the Straight and Narrow Path

Set yourself apart in positive ways from those who walk blithely down the broad way. Every great person's success has in some way found a narrow way, a way others could not or were not willing to go. The poet Robert Frost captured this idea in his poem *The Road Not Taken.*

> *Two roads diverged in a yellow wood,*
> *And sorry I could not travel both*
> *And be one traveler, long I stood*
> *And looked down one as far as I could*
> *To where it bent in the undergrowth;*
>
> *Then took the other, as just as fair,*
> *And having perhaps the better claim,*
> *Because it was grassy and wanted wear;*
> *Though as for that the passing there*
> *Had worn them really about the same,*
>
> *And both that morning equally lay*
> *In leaves no step had trodden black.*
> *Oh, I kept the first for another day!*
> *Yet knowing how way leads on to way,*
> *I doubted if I should ever come back.*
>
> *I shall be telling this with a sigh*
> *Somewhere ages and ages hence:*
> *Two roads diverged in a wood, and I—*
> *I took the one less traveled by,*
> *And that has made all the difference.*

A modern-day example of an extremely successful leader with great integrity is Jon H. Huntsman, Sr. He was born in

Blackfoot, Idaho, into a poor family. He is now the CEO of the world's largest privately held chemical company. In 1987 he agreed to sell "40 percent of Huntsman Corp. for $54 million. By the time the deal closed, that 40 percent was worth $250 million." Not having a legal obligation because there were no contracts signed, Huntsman sold to the buyer for the original amount agreed upon. He said, "I shook your hand and I never want it to be said that I wasn't a man of my word, even if it costs me a lot of additional money." The company now has 16,000 employees and revenues of almost $10 billion and growing.

Huntsman does what he says he will do. He said, "I've found in life that keeping a commitment at all costs is probably the greatest single area of personal carelessness and irresponsibility that people tend to have because they don't think others are listening." He believes that you get what you pay for. He "makes sure his employees get competitive salaries."

> - *Investor's Business Daily*, July 30, 1999. "*Huntsman Corp.'s Jon Huntsman - His Honesty Helped Him Climb to the Top.*"

Stewardship and Delegation

A steward is person who has been given responsibility for someone else or for something belonging to someone else.

Stewardship is the careful, responsible management of something entrusted to one's care. It involves:

1. Entrusting
2. Agency
3. Accountability.

Delegation is to give another person responsibility and authority to accomplish a task for which you are ultimately responsible. Leaders involve others, inspire them, and bless their lives. Offer help and encouragement, but don't make all the decisions for them.

In the *Old Testament*, Moses was a great leader, but after he led the people of Israel out of Egypt he found it difficult to solve all the people's problems by himself. Every day, from morning until evening, he sat before the people to answer their questions and to resolve their difficulties. The task was too much for one man. After receiving counsel from Jethro, his father-in-law, Moses divided the people into groups of 10, 50, 100, and 1,000. He then appointed a reliable man to lead each group.

Thereafter, as the prophet of Israel, Moses spent his time teaching the people the commandments and solving the most difficult problems. The other problems were handled by the leaders he had called Moses became a more effective leader by organizing the people he served. His use of the principles of stewardship and delegation helped him establish order among the people of Israel and govern them more effectively.

In the book, *Get Better or Get Beaten!*, one of the world's most successful business managers, Jack Welch of General Electric, says, "The old organization was built on control, but the world has changed. The world is moving at such a pace that control has become a limitation. It slows you down. You've got to balance freedom with some control, but you've got to have more freedom than you ever dreamed of."

Freedom comes through empowerment and training. A very interesting story is told about one of the best and most efficiently operated organizations in the world. As leader of one of these units, a new president was chosen. But, he accepted the new assignment with some reservations, as he had not had experience in leading such a large organization. He had two counselors serving at his side, who were much like vice presidents in the traditional business organization.

He asked his superior for some advice on how to proceed. His superior's answer was that if he delegated he would do just fine. When the new president asked if he could get some training on the subject, his superior told him to make a complete list of all of his responsibilities and tasks on a single piece of paper. The superior then promised that the next day after the speeches and induction ceremony he would personally give the new president the training he needed. Following the speeches and ceremony, the superior was about to get into the car arranged to take him to catch his flight back to headquarters.

Just a he was about to leave, the expectant president stepped forward and reminded him of his earlier offer and produced the requested list. "Oh yes," said the superior, "It looks like you have done a good job and included almost everything." He tore the paper in half and said, "Give one half to your first counselor and the other to the second. Teach and inspire them, and require them to report on their responsibilities. Keep only the things you cannot delegate to others. That's how you delegate." Then the superior got into his car and rode away.

Make sure you are as free as possible to do the things only you can do. Don't get bogged down in logistical details. Don't get trapped into handling small details.

Definition of Delegation

Webster's New Collegiate Dictionary describes delegation as "the act of empowering." Delegating is equated to the ability to leverage oneself. Delegation is a vital business and leadership skill. Without the ability to delegate one cannot be a leader. In cases it becomes very difficult to carry one some business function. Authority without responsibility is despotism and anarchy.

In the process of delegating it is important to both parties that when a responsibility is given, the authority to carry out that responsibility is also given. Having the responsibility without the authority is a most miserable position to be in. Giving responsibility without authority is most foolish.

Very often when responsibility is given, training is required. Teaching correct principles and leadership training is not only required in order to endow the recipient with knowledge, understanding, and sentiment of responsibility, but it is also required to prevent the recipient from proceeding with authority alone.

Accountability

"An accounting should always be made to the leaders, and he should expect such accounting. . . . This can be a very rewarding experience for both parties, where there is an opportunity to give a self-evaluation, and where communication should be open and constructive. It is an ideal setting for offering and receiving help and assistance."

- N. Eldon Tanner

A Message to Garcia by *Elbert Hubbard, 1899*

A great example of someone who was a dependable steward was Rowan. The battle was raging and to save the day, valuable information needed to be given to General Garcia. Someone said to President McKinley of the United States during the war in Cuba, "There's a fellow by the name of Rowan who will find Garcia for you, if anybody can.' How he did it is not the point. The point is that President McKinley gave Rowan a letter to be delivered to Garcia. Rowan took the letter and did not ask, 'Where is he?'

It is not book-learning young men need, nor instruction about this and that, but a stiffening of the vertebrae which will cause them to be loyal to a trust, to act promptly, concentrate their energies: do the thing, 'Carry a message to Garcia!' General Garcia is dead now, but there are other Garcias."

Part of the story states: "Nothing is said about the employer who grows old before his time in a vain attempt to get frowsy ne'er-do-wells to do intelligent work; and his long patient striving with 'help' that does nothing but loaf when his back is turned. In every store and factory there is a constant weeding-out process going on. The employer is constantly sending away 'help' that have shown their incapacity to further the interests of the business, and others are being taken on. No matter how good times are, this sorting continues, only if times are hard and work is scarce, the sorting is done finer- but out and forever out, the incompetent and unworthy go. It is the survival of the fittest. Self-interest prompts every employer to keep the best – those who can carry a message to Garcia."

"Of course I know that one morally deformed is no less to be pitied than a physical cripple; but in our pitying, let us drop a tear, too, for the men who are striving to carry on a great enterprise, whose working hours are not limited by the whistle, and whose hair is fast turning white through the struggle to hold in line dowdy indifference, slip-shod imbecility, and the heartless ingratitude, which, but for their enterprise, would be both hungry and homeless. . . . My heart goes out to the man who does his work when the "boss" is away, as well as when he is at home."

If you want to be great regardless of your preference or point of interest, always represent others as you would want them to represent you. Be good and be great! Great people are fair to everyone. By being fair to one person, you should not have to worry about what other people think of what you are doing or how you treat them.

Money alone motivates neither the best people, nor the best in people. It can move the body and influence the mind, but it cannot touch the heart or move the spirit; that is reserved for belief, principle, and morality. Values and purpose are the strongest motivators. As Napoleon observed, "No amount of money will induce someone to lay down their life, but they will gladly do so for a bit of yellow ribbon."

Greatest Assets

Other people are most valuable. They can be either our biggest challenge or our greatest asset. Some say it is a "dog eat dog world" or "survival of the fittest" and all that stuff. However, valued friends or employees will be there for you when you need them. They can help you or perform in your presence and cover for you in your absence. Sure you may be taken advantage of on occasion, but that will be the exception rather than the rule.

Treat others right. They will help you be great and they will help you succeed in reaching your goals. You are like the tip of the iceberg that rises above the water line to brave the cold wind or bask in the warm sunshine. Other people represent the unseen mass that keeps you above water supporting and making it all possible.

Occasionally, inexperienced people may not help others develop or give them a chance to shine. We often hold others back because of a fear of losing them. We all remember the best friends and teachers in our lives who loved us, stood by us and gave us the tools, skills, and opportunities to excel and then pushed us to do our best.

Personal service should come ahead of customer service. In fact, our family and friends are our most valuable customers. A great person will support and help to develop others so they will become valuable contributors. It should be taken as a compliment if they go on to do bigger and better things, hopefully with you, but maybe on their own or with others.

Personal relationship turnover can be problematic and even debilitating. In a company, employee turnover can be fatal and is one of the biggest costs in doing business. Some companies with high turnover seem to have an attitude of "turn and burn"! They go through employees who finally get fed up and go elsewhere. Other very successful companies have zero or very low by providing fair salaries, benefits, and training. Great people value personal relationships and nurture them. There is an old adage that says, "Make new friends, but keep the old. The new are like silver and the others like gold."

Don't be Average

Average is the best of the worst and the worst of the best. To be your best, be willing to give your best. To be the best, you must be willing to pay the price. For example, for a company to get the best employees, they should be willing to pay the best salaries. If a business owner pays minimum wages, he or she can expect minimum results.

Sadly, many employers also keep employees working only part time so the business doesn't have to provide benefits. If the original owners of many companies saw what was going on today, they wouldn't stand for it. One such entrepreneur said, "It seems unethical to be getting rich while the troops are making minimum wage and remain unprotected."

Additionally, the older and more mature employees should not be overlooked. Someone with more age experience and gray hair may be more stable and valuable through the startup years. Look around. Large companies now hire older employees who want to be useful and who know how to treat customers right.

Wise entrepreneurs will have good protective systems in place, but they will trust their employees. They know if they have faith in their employees, not fear, they will respond accordingly. Remember the beautiful story of *Les Miserables*. The wise Priest was forgiving and generous. He invested in a man's character and gave him a second chance. Do likewise and remember where it all comes from. Personal relationships and employees are our first and best resource. If you take care of them, they will take care of you.

Dining Delight

Following a delicious banquet and stimulating discussion about how the Goldenmanlou Chain Enterprise, a family-owned-and-operated restaurant chain, could expand their market, I wrote to the General Manager, Zu Hua, and said, "The dining table is often the best place for sharing ideas and for developing plans and meaningful relationships. Like great recipes for delicious and nourishing dishes, ideas and relationships are mixed in the environment of hospitality, seasoned with friendship, warmed with trust, and then shared generously for the benefit of all who partake."

Many business relationships are developed and deals made around the dining table. Wouldn't it be wonderful if the same spirit of hospitality, enjoyment and concern for our guest's satisfaction could carry over into our negotiations and permeate our contracts, production, and conflict resolutions?

Chapter 4

Guiding Greatness

*".God's grace is not the light at the end of the tunnel.
It's the light that guides us through it."*
- Anonymous

"God's grace is helping those who help themselves."
- Anonymous

A Guide

The responsibility of a guide is to not only give answers, but to raise questions, suggest directions to explore, and to offer support to a person reborn of the inspiration from within and from the teacher without.

Years ago a tourist from a big city stopped to ask the old farmer if he was on the road to the city.

The farmer replied, "Dunno, I can't tell ya 'cause I ain't never been thur'."

Puzzled, the tourist asked if this was the Route 99 going south to the state line.

A similar answer came back, "Dunno what its cawlled."

A little frustrated now, the tourist raised his voice and asked, "Will this road take me to the new freeway?"

Again the farmer responded, "Dunno, but the road forks about a mile up ahead".

"Say," said the tourist, "You sure don't know much for a local!"

Turning back to his work, the farmer smiled, spit, and said, "Yeah, you're probably right, but I sure ain't lost."

A guide keeps you from getting lost!

Sometimes, because we are from far away, traveling too fast, or going to new places, we get lost and need simple directions from a knowledgeable source. Oftentimes, we have many alternatives to choose from. The signs are many, the scenery obscure, and so many voices beckon us. In life's travels, an experienced guide is paramount to having a meaningful journey and safe arrival.

Sacagawea, Guide to Lewis and Clark

In 1803, President Thomas Jefferson won approval from Congress for a visionary project, an endeavor that would become one of America's greatest stories of adventure. With the appropriated funds, a small expeditionary group started on a mission to explore the uncharted West and search for a northwest passage to the Pacific Ocean. Meriwether Lewis and his friend William Clark and their large group of men spent the next four years traveling thousands of miles over land and river. They returned with valuable information to help guide the future development of the United States of America. Upon leaving on their expedition they said, "We don't know what we'll find when we get there, but we'll be sure to let you know when we get back."

On the expedition, two French-Canadian fur traders were enlisted to replace original members of the party. One of these men brought his teenage Shoshone Indian wife, Sacagawea, and their infant son, Pomp. Years Sacagawea had been kidnapped by an enemy tribe and taken from her home in Idaho to North Dakota. There she was sold as a slave to a fur trader who took her as his wife.

On the trip, Sacagawea interpreted for the explorers and Indians they met. She helped guide the group and found food and wild medicines. On one occasion, when her boat almost capsized, she displayed her normal calmness under duress and saved valuable documents. Sacagawea turned out to be incredibly valuable to the party as it traveled westward through the territories of many Indian tribes. Her vote in expedition decisions was counted equally with those of the captains and other men.

On the return journey, Sacagawea proved to be a valuable guide through her homeland. The expedition traveled over trails she remembered from her childhood. They returned to her husband's home in August, 1806. Sacagawea received nothing for her contributions, but her husband received some money and land. She gave birth to a daughter six years after the expedition and died at age twenty-five.

Dimensions of Greatness

There are many aspects, or dimensions, of greatness. Very often it is equated with leadership or bringing about change, significant achievement, or excellence in a specific area. These are all valid aspects of greatness and demand notice, prestige, and reward. However, even though they are very important aspects of greatness, they are only a part.

You can become great by starting where you are, developing your character and building on your strengths. You can focus on results and developing others. The secret to building greatness is to become excellent in this powerful combination of skills.

Orchestra

If we combine many talents and skills we can enhance our greatness. Individual instruments can create beauty and inspire the divine. But an orchestra can play the whole symphony. At different times in our lives, we perfect skills with violins, pianos, or drums, but these alone cannot play a symphony. The orchestra plays a symphony with combined notes and chords and movements of many instruments performing in harmony and precision. Similarly, individuals can learn to manage and balance the many attributes, talents, qualities, skills, and habits that make up who they are and not just what they do.

What Individuals Do to Become Great Leaders

Because the past is the best predictor of the future, a probing analysis of people's past does strongly predict their future, and leadership patterns are often established early in life. Hard work, persistence, zeal to learn, a willingness to extend beyond one's comfort zone, tenacity (and possibly luck) enable many to succeed.

Focus

Identify the most important goals for you and your organization. Work to break the urgency addiction and focus on priorities. With practice, greatness can become a choice. Actions that unleash human potential follow such choices.

The key to unleashing individual human potential is about instilling principles into the hearts and minds of people, then into the culture, where the principles begin to permeate and affect everyone. This inspires people to commit to a common vision, a common purpose, and a common set of principles, thereby giving a clear sense of direction. This is the surest way to create strength and success in today's world.

Often people say they possess far more creativity, resourcefulness, ingenuity, intelligence, and talent than their jobs require or even allow.

There is a high cost of low trust. Most organizations have no means of measuring its bottom-line impact. There is little motivation to seriously address it. Employees feel like helpless victims of the problems in their organizations and see no clear way to influence their leaders. However, there are specific and powerful things you can do that will profoundly impact the level of trust in your relationships, your team, your family, and your organization. Every activity, including exploring, training and development all demonstrate measurable growth and value added.

Total Personal Makeover

Dave Ramsey wrote a bestselling book titled, *Total Money Makeover*. It would be great if this book, written to help people get out of debt and live a prosperous life, could serve as a "Total Personal Makeover," outlining a step-by-step process of: 1) finding or being introduced to truth; 2) investigating and testing true personal change and development by following truth and the good example of others. This book is more than just a knowledge-based guidebook. It is also a "how to" book outlining the various steps of gaining knowledge, changing behavior, developing, and progressing. It can have a dramatic effect on helping people in all aspects of their lives.

Chapter 5

Relationship Governed

"Do unto others as you would have them do unto you."
- Golden Rule

My father taught me to be kind to everyone, but choose your friends wisely. He said, "Associate with good people and be careful with what you want because you will probably get it." I interpreted this to mean that I should help others in need and to help each person to be their best. I also came to understand that we tend to rise to the expectations of others so it is important that our friends are good role models and bring out the best in us. I won't use personal examples to emphasize these principles here for extrapolation into professional or intellectual world situations. Instead, I will try to use some familiar business examples of greatness that can be extrapolated into our personal lives.

Establish Authority

No successful organization is ever built or maintained without strong ultimate authority. Participatory decision making is good to an extent, but only when there is real, ultimate, final authority at the top. Be sure there is no doubt about where the buck stops in your organization. Know the extent of your authority and exercise it. This does not negate the wise practice of an open door policy of feedback or sharing of ideas etc.

This is about responsibility and it applies in business and in our personal lives. One of the most famous examples is that of U.S. President Harry Truman who relied on his aids and top advisors for the best intelligence available, but at the end of the day he said, "The buck stops here!"

Build on Strengths

There is wisdom in studying greatness to learn about greatness. Spend your time with great people. Watch and learn from them. Become articulate in describing greatness. Relationships built on strengths will last. No matter how well intended, relationships preoccupied with weaknesses never end well.

Develop alliances and trust others. Start where you are and work with the resources you have. Don't let present circumstances get in the way of future possibilities! Time away from your best is alarmingly destructive. We are wired to need attention, and if we are not getting attention, we tend to change our behavior until we do.

Focus on your strengths and manage around your weaknesses. One of the signs of greatness is the ability to describe, in detail, your unique talents and those of others. Try to highlight and perfect each person's unique style. Run interference for others and help each other be superstars. Treat each person as he or she would like to be treated. Fairness does not mean sameness.

The language of "average" is pervasive. "Quota" means an acceptable level of performance. Don't use average to estimate the limits of excellence. Don't use average performance as a barometer against which a person's performance is judged. Average thinking actively limits performance, and you will drastically underestimate what is possible.

Greatness is achieved through a never-ending pursuit of improvement in all areas. Select a few areas, and when you have developed in those areas, move on to others. Be committed to your own standards and stay focused. Be persistent every day, and determined over the long run.

Discover what ignites your passion and the passion of those around you. We should only pursue those ideas and goals we can get passionate about.

Parable of the Best Talents

A manager asked the HR Specialist what he had to do to become a great leader. The HR Specialist answered, "There was once a man who had two sons. They were both well-educated and prepared to enter the professional world. Both were intelligent and skilled and had the necessary talents required to becoming great leaders among the people. Both had great potential, but did not excel in talent. However, neither was significantly deficient in any area. The father counseled them both to be humble and obedient and to develop their talents and stand above the crowd in order to excel and be perceived as a great leader.

"One son thought in his heart to select his two or three strongest talents and to work and focus on them every day to develop them to excellence and greatness. This he did faithfully for the next five years.

"The other son also took his father's counsel seriously. However, he was determined to improve on his two or three weakest traits in order to eliminate them. He too diligently focused much thought and great energy and effort in order to progress.

49

"Both sons achieved their goals and felt good about their individual progress. The first son seemed to have great luck and always found himself in the right place at the right time to take advantage of and benefit from opportunities that just seemed to come his way. On the other hand, good fortune seemed to elude the second son, who began to think that life was too hard and often unfair."

The wise HR Specialist asked the manager which brother would the people choose when they came together to select their leader. The manager replied, "The first son, of course."

"Very well," said the HR Specialist, "Now go and do likewise. It is always easier to climb when looking up, and remember that you will win the race by riding the stallion, not the donkey."

The Right Person and the Right Job

Be the right person for the job and find the right job for you. In his book *Good to Great,* Jim Collins teaches that great people and organizations get themselves and their people on the right bus and in the right seat. Great people create opportunities. They focus on getting the right people in the right places to make the greatest contributions. The "right person" has more to do with character traits and innate abilities than specific knowledge, background, or skills. Hire the right people so you only need to manage the system, not the people.

For example, you may have the greatest mechanic in the world selling your product. But if that mechanic doesn't know the features and benefits the customers are looking for then he won't sell many cars. On the other hand, if you have the best car salesman in the garage, but if he doesn't know how to change out an engine, transmission or brakes then he won't be a successful mechanic.

Collins writes that many employees consistently perform less than spectacularly in business, even with their ivy-league educations. If you are hiring, look long and hard at the results the person has produced. Begin with who, rather than what. You build a great organization by "injecting an endless stream of talent" directly into the veins of that organization. Average people are trained to quietly submit to dictates of domineering leaders and always wait to see which way the wind blows. The right people will "self-motivate." Get the right people on the bus, the wrong people off the bus, and the right people in the right seats – and then figure out where to drive the bus. The right people are your most important assets.

When you have selected the right people give them clear direction and assignments along with the authority and responsibility to do their job. Then hold them accountable and reward them appropriately. It's who you pay, not how you pay them. You can teach farmers how to make steel, but it's difficult to teach a person a strong work ethic if he doesn't have it in the first place. "We hire five, work them like ten and pay them like eight." To continue with Collins' analogy, create an environment where hardworking people will thrive and lazy people will either jump or get thrown off the bus.

Hire Employees with Character

When hiring employees, place greater weight on character attributes than on specific educational background, practical skills, specialized knowledge, or work experience. These things are all teachable or obtainable. However, attributes of character, work ethic, basic intelligence, dedication, commitment, and values are ingrained. We want to know: Who are they? Why are they? Why did they make the decisions in life that they made? The best hiring decisions often come from people with no industry or business experience.

The best people need not worry about their positions and can concentrate fully on their work. "The only way to help to the people who are achieving is to not burden them with the people who are not achieving." Giving second chances is like subjecting your culture to the death of a thousand cuts. Deal with problems right up front. Rigor in a good-to-great company applies first at the top, focused on those who hold the largest burden of responsibility. These companies seldom use head-count layoffs as a tactic and almost never used it as a primary strategy. Lesser companies used the chronic addition of layoffs five times more frequently, causing endless restructuring and mindless hacking.

When in doubt, don't hire – keep looking. When you know you need to make a people change, act. The best people don't need to be managed. Letting the wrong people hang around is unfair to all the right people. It can drive away the best people. Get rid of them or move them to a position where they can blossom. Put your best people on your biggest opportunities, not your biggest problems. Be one who spends almost all your waking hours with people you love, who all love what you and they are doing, and who love one another.

What Bus and What Seat?

Allow me to continue to use Jim Collin's analogy of getting the right people on the bus and into the right seat from his book *Good to Great*. You might ask, "How do I know what bus to get on and what is the best seat for me?" Well, you need to be asking what you enjoy the most, what brought you to this point in your life and what keeps you here. You must know your strengths and weaknesses and have clearly defined values and goals. Be serious, analytical, and documented about answering these questions. It will be revealed to you in how you answer these questions. Past choices and behavior is predictive of your future.

If you choose the seat of a leader or manager, make sure you have the right tools. You need the right to build your own immediate staff. Be sure to pick the right people. Choose your closest associates, and allow those you hire to do the same thing. Do not hire or promote your own image that will duplicate your strengths and weaknesses. Each employee should report to only one boss.

Provide training and development opportunities and evaluate employees monthly and annually. Trust them, but don't over-promote them. Reward them well for what they do. Never pass the buck. Make very few promises to your people, and keep them all. You are on stage every day.

When firing an employee, do it fast. You are entrusted with the health of the enterprise, so you must constantly cut and prune. Your team is vital to your success and the success of your organization.

Managing with Tough Love

The art of tough love is removing someone from his or her role the right way. Managers must know:

1. What level of performance is unacceptable?
2. How long is too long at that level?

Have you done enough to help with training, motivation, support systems, or complementary partnering? Working this way forces mangers to confront poor performance early, but allows them to do so in such a way that much of the bitterness or bad feelings disappear. In the minds of great managers, consistent poor performance is not primarily a matter of weakness, stupidity, disobedience, or disrespect. It is a matter of miscasting. Don't participate in assisted career suicide. Get employees into a position that is right for them, not what they might want at the time.

Collins says, "Hire and promote first on the basis of integrity; second, motivation; third, capacity; fourth, understanding; fifth, knowledge; and last and least, experience. Without integrity, motivation is dangerous; without motivation, capacity is impotent; without capacity, understanding is limited; without understanding, knowledge is meaningless; without knowledge, experience is blind. Experience is easy to provide and quickly put to good use by people with all other qualities."

Having said and quoted all of this, I now challenge you, the reader, to apply these ideas and principles in your personal life by asking yourself, "Am I on the right bus? What is the right bus for me and how do I find it and how do I get on it and once I'm on it how do I find the right seat for me? Am I in the right seat now? If not, which is the right seat for me and how do I switch?"

These are tough questions and may require some tough choices and changes. Regular personal inventory is good and will bring good results. This is what great people do. Measure where you are, what you are doing and where you are going against your personal mission statement, values and goals. At periodic crossroads in your life, this can be the highest and best use of your time. If you do this, I promise great results!

Talents, Skills, and Knowledge

Don't confuse talents with skills and knowledge. Skills are how you do things. Knowledge is what facts you are aware of. Talents are your patterns of thought, feeling, or behavior. There are how you strive, think, and relate. Skills and knowledge can be acquired and developed, but your talents will remain stable, familiar to you and to others throughout your life. They are your habits and attitudes and drive. When looking for greatness in hiring, hunt for talent before looking for experience or knowledge. When developing greatness in yourself, trust in and develop your talents while gaining experience and knowledge.

Jon Huntsman defined this in greater detail. He admonished that you must know exactly what talents you are looking for and be able to recognize it when you find it. You must hire well and train well. "Then the next thing you do is give them a lot of rope, a lot of authority, and test them. Make them an entrepreneur in their own right. Don't make decisions for them." As a leader, be out and about and working with your team. "You can't motivate people by sitting behind a desk. You've got to be out cheering your troops. This means being out where they are and shaking their hands and thanking them."

In all his business dealings, Huntsman does thorough research and follows his heart in all his negotiations. He said, "You do all negotiations by emotion. You don't do them by logic. Emotions are very critical in negotiations and life in general." In dealing with competitors or partners, he tries to develop good relations. "We try to have friendship blossom into romance, not unlike between a husband and wife. You get close to them and find out what it is that is their driving factor, and you try to accommodate that."

Celebrating and Rewarding Others

Praise others, share the glory and give credit where credit is due. Praise others publicly. Be generous with gratitude. In business as well as in all aspects of life, it is impossible to say "thank you" too many times. Keep in touch with people leading traditional, normal lives. There is greatness in everyone. There is heroism in everyone.

It is common knowledge that the Sea World killer whales have been trained to perform great feats while displaying delight in their behavior. It is an example of the power of positive relationships and the need to catch people doing things right. Too often we are trying to catch people doing things wrong. Reward is the secret of training killer whales. Each time the killer whale performs correctly, they are rewarded with a fish. Punishment does not work and is life threatening. Punishment is also harmful in human relationships. Whale training and people training uses the same process and teaching.

Everything is based on and driven by our positive relationships. Don't ever punish others. As managers at home or at work we all are motivating others in one way or another. Pay attention to your interactions with others. Build positive relationships to increase people's energy and improve their performance. It's all about what you focus on. It feels good to focus on the bright and noble and wonderful in people.

Accentuate the Positive

Accentuating the positive and focusing energy toward a positive outcome always works best. Ignore what others do wrong and immediately redirect their behavior elsewhere. The more attention you pay to a behavior, the more it will be repeated, whether good behavior or bad. It's what you focus on that is the key. Accentuate the positive, not just to get performance, but because it's the right thing to do. Persuade others see us as their friends. After friendship is established, then study the other person's behavior and find out what she likes. Make everything in their training a fun game.

The most harmful practices in education are to mentally limit others. What we think about others and expect from them has a direct bearing on that person's response or lack of response. The conventional approach is one of a "superior" being compelling an "inferior" being to do what the teacher wants done. People can sense expectations with astonishing accuracy and will "live up or down" to others' expectations. Always expect the best. Expect the impossible!

Introduction Exercise

First, greet people around you as if they're not important, and you're looking for someone else more important to talk to. Not much really happens. Then, greet everyone around you as if they're long lost friends and you're so glad to see them. Instantly the place will become alive with movement and loud voices. To motivate people you have to know how to manage people's energy. You increase the energy by changing what you focus your attention on.

ABC's of Performance

The ABC's of performance are described by activators, behavior, and consequences. People need to know what they are being asked to do. Our activators are goals that clarify our understanding. Our behavior, or performance, is motivated by these goals. Training helps everyone know how to achieve the goals. The consequence of our behavior is the response that people give and has the greatest impact on our performance.

When working with others in a leadership or family role, there can be positive or negative responses or no response at all. There can also be redirection responses. Negative and no response are not productive in improving performance. Effective redirection by immediately refocusing energies elsewhere should follow without blame. When mistakes occur, redirect the energy. The positive response in the form of praise, learning opportunities, or promotion is the best way to promote greatness.

Praise progress. Catch people doing things better and praise the behavior. Set others up for success. Catching people doing things wrong is easy. There is a ripple effect of this "GOTcha" response. The boss yells at one of his managers, who yells at his associate, who goes home and yells at his spouse, who yells at the child, who kicks the cat. Everyone is hoping to be caught doing something right and being rewarded with a positive response. Let people show you what they are doing right, and then praise them for it. When you accentuate the positive, you'll begin to pay attention to what you do or say after people perform. I guarantee their performance will improve, and so will your relationship.

A negative response is a last resort. Tell people immediately and specifically what they did that was unacceptable—including the negative impact of their action and how you feel about it. Always end that kind of message with an affirmation of the person. They need to know that it's the behavior, not them personally, that you find unacceptable.

People aren't whales, always seeking rewards. They have minds and act in ways they think are good and acceptable. Finding out what motivates people is important. You don't want people to become dependent solely on your noticing, commenting, and rewarding. Learn to influence people to do the right thing when you are not around. Instead of building dependency on others for a reward, you want people to do the right things because they themselves enjoy it. Help people become self-motivating by catching themselves doing things right, and then acting accordingly. You can say, "I'll bet that felt good" or "You must be proud of . . . ." or "Tell me how that feels". Positive response is not an end in itself. It's a lead-up to the ultimate goal of helping people catch themselves doing things right.

You have an impact on people's performance even when you ignore them. Individuals are motivated by different things in the short term (day to day) and in the long term (monthly, quarterly, yearly, etc.). Never assume you know what motivates a person. To find out, ASK sincerely. They will feel your sincerity. Don't blow smoke or polish the apple. People can see right through phony praise. This breeds mediocrity. Positive praise only works when you're sincere and honest.

Parenting and Marriage

This process can help you be more proactive about parenting. If the baby is not in distress, it may be better to pick up the baby when she stops fussing and cuddle her then, not just when she is crying. Watch when small children are getting bored and restless and redirect their energy before they start to fight and get into trouble. Create an environment where they know good things happen when they are "taking care of business".

In marriage, if you continue to recognize good behavior, this approach can go a long way to building happy families. We naturally want approval from others. "Love is blind" means that when you first fall in love, all you see is the positive. After you are married you notice all those things about your partner that you were blind to in the beginning.

The final demise of a love relationship is when you do something right and you still get yelled at because you didn't do it right enough. The question is, do you want the relationship to work? Once committed, you can take on any problem if you are both committed to your mutual commitment. Periodically, renew your commitment and expressions of love.

Don't be hard on others because you are hard on yourself or someone else is hard on you. Look at every individual as a winner. Trust others and have faith that focusing on positive behavior works. Help build everyone and they will build each other. It's fun to be around people who like themselves.

Giving

Greatness is giving. The essence is not giving things, but giving of oneself and one's spirit. Material gifts *are* important— the gifts of self will often take material forms. The quest of greatness is a journey to find the treasure of true self and transform your own life and then to to give your treasure to transform the world.

Caring begins with knowing about others—it requires listening. Caring is the willingness to reach out and open one's heart. An open heart is vulnerable. Accepting vulnerability allows us to drop our masks, meet heart to heart, and be present for one another. Love is largely absent in modern corporations. At work, and in other groups, we pretend to love others and they pretend to love us.

Power Promotes Productivity

Stripped of power, people look for ways to fight back with sabotage, passive resistance, withdrawal, or angry militancy. Giving power liberates energy for more productive use. When people feel a sense of efficacy and an ability to influence their world, they seek to be productive.

The gift of power is closely linked to conflict. When power is hoarded and centralized, conflict is often suppressed. Tyrannical parents, leaders or governments tend to take away freedoms and options of expression. Feeling powerless, seeing their parents as the enemy, young people try to empower themselves through gangs and guns. Feeling the same, disgruntled employees will become disengaged and may even sabotage their company or organization. Suppressed citizens will revolt and fight for freedom and power.

Effective parents and leadership give power without undermining the family's or system's integrity, making it possible to confront conflict without confrontation, violence or warfare. A family or community is a group that fights gracefully. Ritual and ceremony help us experience the unseen webs of significance that tie a community together. Family or city councils are convened on a regular basis to discuss various needs and disputes. A process of negotiation, resolution and decision is agreed upon and followed.

Seek Fair Results for All Parties

It is possible to live and work in a world where we can cheer for the success of others and not just measure our success by their defeat? In a way, however, the rough and tumble world of business and life in general is like a sport and entrepreneurs are like athletes. There is a need to be physically fit and mentally prepared in order to understand the rules, practice the skills, and do your best to win. There are the obvious scenarios of Win – Lose, Lose – Lose, Win – Win. Under normal circumstances great people will strive for the Win – Win scenario.

Except in sporting events, no one wants to be in a win – lose or lose – lose scenario. There is no reason why we should not want to seek a fair and equitable win – win result in almost every situation. This is in keeping with an abundance mentality which is another quality of greatness.

Negotiating

To be an effective negotiator, we need to have perception and intuition, patience and flexibility. We must be personal and professional and give attention to detail. Negotiating is all about giving and getting. Negotiating is the process of solving problems and requires a mutual search for solutions. We must know the difference between negotiating and confrontation. If our thinking is if/then, we are negotiating. If our thinking is either/o,r we are confronting.

We need to always ask, "You have told me what you want, now tell me what you need." Everyone needs leverage. Everyone has objectives. The simplest part of the negotiating process is establishing what you want to get, what you are willing to give up, and when you will do so.

The traditional steps of negotiating transactions include introductions, reviewing background and objectives, creating an appropriate environment, communication, identifying issues, resolving issues or conflicts, compromise and settlement. Finally, there is post settlement, where all parties comply with the results.

These steps apply in negotiating with your spouse, child, boss or head of state. Understanding the process and where you are makes a big difference in the immediate success and long-term outcome.

We negotiate in all areas of our lives. Great people develop negotiation styles and preferences. Practice this skill as you would any other skill, and remember that you are always negotiating with someone else or with yourself.

Financial Capabilities

Great people understand and live by basic principles of personal prosperity. It's easier to become wealthy than to endure poverty. There are, however, definitely more people who desire wealth than have it. To accomplish future goals and to realize desires one must learn and understand how to make and manage money. There are fundamental rules and principles of personal prosperity that are timeless

Being proactive and doing good and honest work will provide a multitude of opportunities to make money. In business decisions, trust in your first impressions and be proactive in taking advantage of opportunity.

Procrastination and gambling will rob a person of their wealth. While gambling is attractive and encouraged by government and society, it will almost always bring loss and will close doors to opportunities. It has been said that it is almost as difficult to retain wealth as to earn it in the first place. Easy come, easy go. Over time, hard-earned wealth needs to be managed with steadiness and purpose.

Great people pay their taxes. Enjoyment of paying taxes is not the issue, but obedience to the law is. Don't pay more taxes than you have to, but pay all you owe.

When investing money, seek expert counsel from wise people who are experts in their field of investments. Carefully measure your risk and your desired return. Invest wisely, with great caution, and don't be tempted to try to "get rich quick". The money we spend today gives us only the things of the moment, but the money we save and invest will grow and provide additional income and enjoyment for the future.

Once you understand and are utilizing these principles for your own benefit, it is important to share the principles of prosperity with others. The prosperity of any nation depends on the prosperity of its individual citizens. Wealth is power, and with this power great achievements are possible. We must know the laws that govern prosperity. If we are not prosperous, it is because we do not understand these laws or we do not obey them.

Now we ask, what are the "Laws of Wealth"? They are true and simple, but then the truth is always simple. They are:

1. Many believing people pay a tithe to their church. They also give generous offerings to their favorite charity. Give first and it will come back in buckets. Often the poor are greedier than the rich. It's like the man sitting in front of the pot belly stove saying, "You give me some heat and I'll put some wood in."

2. Budget and control your expenditures. Do not spend more than you earn. Avoid getting into debt. Debt is your enemy and can defeat you. A part of all we earn is ours to keep. Pay at least 10 percent of

your income to yourself, to be used for savings and investments, before you pay for necessities such as food, home, car, entertainment, etc.

3. Increase your ability to earn by gaining additional education and work experience. Insure against tragedy or death by buying adequate health and life insurance. Keep a supply of food, clothing, fuel, medicines, cash, etc. Insure an income for the future by investing wisely. Make your home a profitable investment.

4. Take advantage of opportunity and do not procrastinate. Taking risks is part of life and an important part of prosperity. Learn to manage risk. Make up your mind and be decisive. Learn to make money and take advantage of opportunities. Being able to know when to make quick decisions is an important skill. Keep going. Don't quit. Take risk only after careful consideration, but do not gamble. Have faith, be honest, work hard, work smart, and endure to the end.

5. Education is the foundation of success. Just as scholastic skills are vitally important, so are financial and communication skills. Schools focus on scholastic and professional skills, but not on financial skills. It is up to you to increase the financial skills of your family.

6. You must know the difference between an asset and a liability, and buy only assets. Real assets are investments or businesses that don't require your presence. If you have to do regular work on the asset or in the business then it's not an asset, it's a job. An asset produces income and appreciates without you having to work at it. They have ready market value.

7. Net worth is not accurate because when you begin selling your assets you are taxed for any gains. Many assets, such as jewelry, vehicles, mobile homes and furniture can only be sold for a fraction of their purchase price or appraised value. Net worth is often worth less than you think. Most assets like cars and personal items depreciate the moment you purchase them.

Great people will learn and live by the sound financial principles and practices. They will strive to prosper by moving from day to day or paycheck to paycheck to investing in the future. They will spend less than they make so they can plant seeds of prosperity that will grow over time into assets that will produce benefits to not only provide for their own needs, but to bless others who are struggling to follow in their footsteps.

Respect and Dignity

A great person will always stand up for others. Acknowledge an honest error without degrading the person unfortunate enough to have made the mistake. Build loyalty and camaraderie. Be quick to forgive and forget.

It is almost impossible to put a value on a loyal friend or employee. In turn, we need to be loyal to our family members, friends, employees and customers. If there is a high level of loyalty then others will respect us and not neglect us in our time of need.

Respect is like air. If you take it away, it's all people can think about. People will do anything to defend their dignity. Honor and regard another person's basic humanity. Respect others and have a sense of mutual purpose.

An apology is a statement that sincerely expresses sorrow for our role in causing or not preventing pain or difficulty to others. We must be sincere and honest in correcting unintended insults. Contrasting or explaining is not apologizing. Forgiveness is not about pretending that bad things didn't happen, it is dealing with situations as they are in a respectful manner and letting go of resentment.

Parable of the Prodigal Partner

Then he said, "A certain man had two junior partners and the younger of them said to the senior partner, "Give me my share, I'm outta' here." So he divided unto them their percentages.

Soon after, the younger partner left and went out to start up a new competitive company and there used all his capital. When he had invested everything, there was a downturn in the economy; and he lost everything. He then teamed up with some other entrepreneurs who put him to work on an hourly basis. He would have rather been struggling to build his own company, but now he was stuck.

He finally got his head together and said, "All of my old partner's employees have benefits and stock options, but here, I have nothing at all. I'm going back to my old partner, and tell him, 'I've been a real jerk to you and everyone else and I'm not worthy of being your partner.'"

He got up the courage and went back, but when he was just coming through the door, his old senior partner saw him, and felt sorry for him, and ran to give him a big hug and a warm welcome. The younger man said, "Partner, I've been terrible to you and everyone else here. I'm not worthy of being your partner." But the senior partner said to his assistants, "Pull the company car around front, get him a credit card, and put him on an expense account. Break out the petty cash and let's have a party. My former partner was a competitor and now he's one of us again; he defected, but now he's straightened himself out, so let's put this all behind us and have a good time."

Now the other junior partner was back in the warehouse. As he came into the office, he heard loud music and saw dancing. He asked one of the security guards what was going on. The guard said, "Your old junior partner has returned; and the boss is putting on the dog for him, because he wants back into the company." This ticked off the other junior partner, and he would not go in.

Then the senior partner came out and tried to coax him in, but the junior partner answered, "Hey man, I've busted my buns for the last ten months and never bailed on you, but you never threw me a gig like this. But as soon as this clown shows up you welcome him back with open arms.

The senior partner answered, "Partner, you've always been here for me and you'll get my share of the company when I'm gone. We should be happy because our former partner has returned with his valuable human and intellectual capital. We're much better off with him than without him, and we only have to pay him an hourly wage. Why not give him a chance?"

We are all responsible for our choices. Some choices bring drastic and sometimes damaging results which require us to live with the consequences of our choices. If we choose to stay on higher ground, we can help others.

A Compliment to Their Team

Many professional sports teams have "superstars" playing for them. At times there are several superstars on the same team. However, no matter how good the individuals are, unless they are team players they usually do not succeed.

An obvious example is the bringing together of the Los Angeles Lakers by their coach, Phil Jackson. He is a team player and got the superstars to be team players. The same superstars had lost consecutively in previous years, but with a seasoned and successful coach who brought them together as a team, they won the world championship in his first year. Greatness means being a great coach and a team player.

Today, organizations need self-reliant, self-motivated, self-directed teams. In these turbulent times, leadership and unity are more important than ever. Great people fit well into their organization. Team players tap into their teammate's talent or strengths. They highlight what people are passionate about and add value to the organization. When your strengths and passions intersect with organizational needs, the outcome is always positive for the individual and the organization.

Team players are constantly focused on how they can make a contribution to the organization. Passion is the element most underrated and yet potentially the most critical part of the model. Love, desire, inspiration, and passion are the greatest differences between good team players and great team players.

Serve Others

Serve others in whatever situation or circumstance you are in. Be a good neighbor and friend. Care for your parents. Take care of your employees' children and your customers' children. Others will give their best performance when there are no distracted by family problems. When you befriend or hire someone, you may not want to consider the fact that you have befriended or hired his or her entire family. A scholarship or an internship to a son or daughter or a letter of recommendation for someone goes a long way in helping others. Provide help as you can and if you are an employer, perhaps give a few days off, a leave of absence, or a temporary salary advance.

Take care of people close to you. They can be the biggest challenge and their greatest asset. Some say it is a "dog eat dog world" or "survival of the fittest" and all that stuff. However, valued friends and employees will be there for you when you need them.

Engagement

As you develop greatness, you will find yourself fully engaged in whatever task you undertake or whatever cause you join whether it be a friendship, family, business or war. Getting other people engaged makes a huge difference in their personal life and to the success of the cause or organization they belong to. "Engaged" people use their talents every day, consistently perform at high levels, are naturally innovative, and have high energy and enthusiasm. The "non-engaged" person just meets the basics.

"Actively disengaged" people have low trust, low commitment, and negative attitudes either covertly or overtly. They drag down and innocently or knowingly sabotage their own life and/or the goals and results of the organization in which they work. To resolve this and help someone become engages, it is important to identify their natural talents and match their purpose, values and goals along with their talents with their roles. Then it we can provide the support and resources to allow them to flourish. It is the same principle as giving water, nutrients and sunshine to a plant. People who use their natural talents for self-fulfillment or in their jobs are significantly more productive than others.

Family

To be a successful father or a successful mother is greater than to be a successful business leader or a successful statesman. David O. McKay taught: "The home is the first and most effective place for children to learn the lessons of life: truth, honor, virtue, self-control; the value of education, honest work, and the purpose and privilege of life. Nothing can take the place of home in rearing and teaching children, and no other success can compensate for failure in the home."

Parents are the master teachers. They do their most effective teaching by example. The family circle is the ideal place to demonstrate and develop self-esteem, kindness, forgiveness, faith, and every other virtue. The family circle is also the best organization to counteract selfishness. We should seek to model our family life after self-sacrifice.

There are two ways of spreading light: to be the candle or to be the mirror that reflects it. Parents can be both. Great people should unite and combine their efforts. There is no human relationship more suited to such teachings than a family where parents truly love and give their lives in service to their children. This teaching should help children be more loving and honoring of their parents. It should also help prepare children to be parents themselves. Parents teach their children, and families learn by doing things together.

Know What You Are Willing to Risk in Your Relationships

"I don't necessarily have to like my players and associates, but as the leader I must love them. Love is loyalty, love is teamwork. Love respects the dignity of the individual. This is the strength of any organization."

- Vince Lombardi

There are four definitions of love: encompassing strong affection, warm attachment, attraction based upon sexual feelings, and choice of service. The Greek word *eros* gave rise to erotic or sexual attraction, desire, and craving. Another Greek word *storg'e,* is affection between family members. The Greek word *philos,* or brotherly, reciprocal love, is somewhat of a conditional love where we do good to others if they do good to us. Greeks use the noun *agape* and the verb *agapao'* to describe a more unconditional love rooted in behavior toward others without regard to their due. It is the love of deliberate choice. When Jesus speaks of love in the New Testament, the word *agape'* is used, a love of behavior and choice, not a love of feeling.

We should behave well toward all people. Love is action, not just feelings. Love is not how we feel about others, rather how we behave toward others. George Washington Carver said, "Be kind to others. How far you go in life depends upon your being tender with the young, compassionate with the aged, sympathetic with the striving, and tolerant of the weak and the strong. Someday in your life, you will have been all of these."

In being selfless, we are trying to meet other's needs. We may not always control how we feel about other people, but we can control of how we behave toward others. Be kind, not arrogant, behave well, don't be selfish, don't hold a grudge, celebrate others success, and mourn their defeats. Love is patience, kindness, humility, respectfulness, selflessness, forgiveness, honesty, and commitment. Charity and service better defines the form *agape'* rather than the usual English definition of love.

Chapter 6

Truth Seekers

"Reality is what we take to be true.
What we take to be true is what we believe.
What we believe is based upon our perceptions.
What we perceive depends upon what we look for.
What we look for depends upon what we think.
What we think depends upon what we perceive.
What we perceive determines what we believe.
What we believe determines what we take to be true.
What we take to be true is our reality."

\- Gary Zukav

Ask, Seek, and Knock

The following applies to the most common and humble people as well as to the most sophisticated and wealthy. Some people think they are successful because they are smarter, richer, or stronger than others. While in part they are correct in their assumptions, it is only in part. There is much more to being successful. The greatest people are successful in their personal and business endeavors because they follow the "B-attitudes".

1. Be true to yourself and your family
2. Be honest and without guilt
3. Be a peacemaker and help resolve problems

4. Be good and help others
5. Be humble and recognize that your success is not only your own doing
6. Be wise—seek truth and excellence.

Listen

More important than speaking is listening. Carefully listen to understand others. When other people know their thoughts and feelings are important to you, they will be more open and receptive to your ideas. Don't get into the habit of thinking about what you are going to say next while they are talking. Find out what matters most important to them. They will tell you what you need to know to guide them, serve them, inspire them, and help them to succeed.

Observe body language and unspoken facial messages. When you listen sincerely, you are sending messages of interest and enthusiasm. Don't be afraid of silence. Everyone needs time to think. Remember the lawyer who kept asking the witness to answer his question. The witness apologized, "I'm not a lawyer. I can't talk without thinking."

Don't interrupt people while they are talking. When you feel like you understand, let them know by repeating back what you think they are saying. When you don't understand, ask for clarification. When someone dominates the conversation, you can tactfully take control by getting back to the purpose of the conversation. If you need to, you can assure the other person that you will return to address their questions or concerns.

Listening moves us closer. When you cut people off in mid-sentence it sends bad and disrespectful messages that you have not been listening, you have already formulated your response, you don't value the person or their opinion, or what you have to say is more important. Your feelings of respect must be aligned with your actions. Wherever you are, be there! Great people seem to hang on every word we speak, which makes us feel valued and important.

Many people wrongly assume that listening is a passive process of being silent while another person speaks. We may believe that we are good listeners, but what were are often doing is selectively, making judgments about what is being said, and thinking of ways to end the conversation or redirect the conversation in ways more pleasing to ourselves. We can all think roughly four times faster than others can speak.

Active listening takes place in our head and requires disciplined effort to silence all that internal conversation while we're attempting to listen to another person. It requires a sacrifice, an extension of our self, to block out the noise and truly enter another person's world. Active listening is attempting to see things as the speaker sees them and attempting to feel things as the speaker feels them.

We refer to empathy as being fully present with someone. It does not mean just physically present, but also mentally and emotionally. Listening is probably the greatest opportunity to give attention to others on a daily basis and convey how much we value them. There is a wonderful effect in being listened to and being allowed to express feelings with another person.

There are essentially four ways to communicate: reading, writing, speaking, and listening. We study for years to develop these first three skills in school, but make virtually no effort whatsoever to teach or learn listening skills. This is a skill we need to use most.

The Egyptian pharaoh named Ptahhotep said, "Those who must listen to the pleas and cries of their people should do so patiently. Because the people want attention to what they say even more than the accomplishing for which they came."

There is a legitimate human need to express and be heard. One of the primary ways to love is paying attention to people. Kindness is giving attention, appreciation, and encouragement to others. The core of the human personality is the need to be appreciated. Praise must be sincere.

Learning

"Life is a progressive process of finding out who we really are and succeeding at whatever we can conceive." Never stop learning. Get all the formal education you can as early as you can. Build into your personal life plan sufficient time and budget for personal training and development.

"Training is expensive, but not as costly as ignorance." Don't sell yourself short. Get all the education you can while you are able. Never stop learning and never stop teaching. You will grow in the process.

Move Ideas from Your Head to the Market

"Everything that can be invented, has been invented."
- U.S. Patent Office Director, 1899

If you are a parent, school teacher, fireman, civil servant, waiter/waitress, a pilot or a police officer, can you apply the following to your personal life?

Parable of the Trainer

And when all the employees and upper management were met together and were come to the training seminar out of every department. The Director spoke by a parable:

"A trainer went out to teach his seminar: and as he taught, some ideas and principles fell on deaf ears; and it was not received, but rejected and competition came in and 'ate their lunch' and stole away their clients.

"And some ideas and principles fell upon eager ears; and as soon as it was accepted, it was forgotten because they lacked management support.

"And some fell among pessimists, and criticism sprang up and choked out these good ideas and principles.

"And others fell on prepared ears of those who immediately applied what they had learned and put these principles and ideas into practice. They taught them to those their peers and subordinates and had great success with 100 percent increase in production."

When the Director had said these things, he shouted, "If you want to learn, then listen up."

The Director's management team asked him, saying, "What do you mean with this story?"

He replied, "You are my leaders and have been trained to build this company. Some people just don't get it. But this story is about your responsibility for training and developing each other. People are the company's lifeblood. Those of you who reject or neglect your responsibility are doing more to destroy than to develop. You who are cynical or negative are no better than they because you rob others of vision and enthusiasm of those you work with or those you lead.

"Some of you get excited about training and development, but because of your selfish concerns you don't do anything about it. You don't develop yourself or others. The bottom line for you is that we are wasting your time and our resources.

"Now, there are some of you who are not fully engaged, and the competition is trying to recruit you away from us, and you're tempted to go. You discourage others and prevent them from progressing. Because you are so focused on what you can get from the company, your contributions are small.

"Many of you have your head on straight and your personal priorities in order. You're honest and loyal, and you make things happen by doing everything you can to learn, improve and walk the talk.

"You do this in all aspects of your life. By so doing you benefit our company, your family, your church and your community.

"When the year-end performance appraisal reviews are completed, it will be you who will get raises and bonuses, and the others will get fired."

Think Positively – Be Optimistic

"No pessimist ever discovered the secrets of the stars, or sailed to an unchartered land, or opened a new haven to the human spirit."
- Helen Keller

"Your mind is a 'thought factory.' It's a busy factory, producing countless thoughts in one day. Production in your thought factory is under the charge of two foremen, one of whom we will call Mr. Triumph and the other Mr. Defeat. Mr. Triumph is in charge of manufacturing positive thoughts. He specializes in producing reasons why you can, why you're qualified, why you will. The other foreman, Mr. Defeat, produces negative, depreciating thoughts. He is your expert in developing reasons why you can't, why you're weak, why you're inadequate. His specialty is the 'why-you-will-fail' chain of thoughts. Both Mr. Triumph and Mr. Defeat are intensely obedient. They snap to attention immediately. All you need do to signal either foeman is to give the slightest mental beck-and-call. If the signal is positive, Mr. Triumph will step forward and go to work. Likewise, a negative signal brings Mr. Defeat forward."

   - David J. Schwartz, *The Magic of Thinking Big*

In his book, *See You at the Top*, Zig Ziglar says, ". . . the world's most deadly disease is 'Hardening of the Attitudes.'"

Our success and happiness is largely determined by how we feel about ourselves and others and the world around us. How we feel is determined by how we think and reason.

In his book, *As a Man Thinketh*, James Allen states, "Your attitude is more important than your mental capacity." It's your *attitude* that determines your *altitude*, not how big or smart or how beautiful you are or whether you have lots of money or political influence.

Knowing this we can determine our own destiny.

As Wilford Gardner said, "We must be a thermostat instead of a thermometer." We should regulate and direct our lives and not just reflex to what is happening.

Paul H. Dunn said, "There are three kinds of people: 1) Those few who make things happen, 2) the many who just watch things happen and 3) a whole lot of people who wonder what happened!"

We can and should be like the few who make things happen.

The poet McLandburgh Wilson wrote, "T'wixt optimist and pessimist, the difference is droll, the optimist sees the doughnut; the pessimist, the hole. Two men looked out through the selfsame bars, one saw mud, and the other saw stars."

The philosopher Ralph Waldo Emerson wrote, "Many people see things as they are and ask why? Others see things as they can be and ask why not?"

Cervantes, the great winter and author of <u>Don Quixote</u>, wrote, "Man should see the world, not as it is, but as it should be." We must always have a positive attitude. It depends on our choice of thoughts.

To help me understand this better, I wrote the following poem called "Common Thought":

> *It's a common thing to think a thought*
> *- Of things we are and things we're not.*
> *In deep despair one starts to sink*
> *- If we entertain such thoughts to think.*
> *But if we change the way we think*
> *- Will always rise and never sink*
> *We'll create our world and love a lot,*
> *- For such is born in common thought.*

Abundance versus Scarcity

Occasionally, there have been unique circumstances and individuals who have adopted a approach to wealth called the abundance mentality. Instead of the traditional competitive mindset, they believe that there is enough and more for everyone. There is no scarcity in ideas, natural resources, and opportunities to prosper and resolve problems. This abundance mentality is founded on the notion that the each individual's prosperity is enhanced by helping others achieve what they desire. It suggests that competition is good, but working together is better.

When we think of success in the business world, we tend to think first of the billionaires, multi-millionaires, and top executives as those being great or successful. We are conditioned to think that the masses of average workers are only trading their time for money. These first two groups are considered the givers. Then we might think of the takers as the unemployed, those living in poverty, and the criminals. We have this perception that the riches only go to the smartest, the strongest, and wealthiest.

Many believe that the business marketplace is a jungle where only the fittest survive. It's only the biggest and the best who count and it is all important to be #1. This traditional business mentality has been accepted and perpetuated throughout the history of mankind. The explorers discovered, conquered, or dominated and colonized. Freedom and economic growth were achieved only by throwing off the tyranny or oppression of others. Sadly, the liberators too often became equal to those they replaced and the masses remained as before.

An abundance mentality is very different from a scarcity mentality. Abundance reflects hope and progress. Scarcity reflects doubt and retreat. Abundance promotes progress and sharing. Scarcity promotes decline and selfishness. The mind, the world and the universe is abundant and more!

Common sense dictates that the benefactors of those practicing the B-attitudes or the abundance mentality do not enable others to take advantage or be lazy. The idea is to help others to help themselves. Then the helper will prosper from their efforts. There is wisdom in the ancient Chinese proverb that states, "Give a man a fish and he will ask for more. Teach a man to fish and he will feed a nation."

Accept Responsibility and Act on It

"If it is to be, it is up to me." Those ten two-letter words sum it up best. You should accept absolute responsibility for your life and your success. Because, you must know, it's not luck, fate, the stars, heredity, circumstances, the economy, the weather, your spouse, your parents, or your boss. It is you! You are responsible for what you are and what you will become. To many people, that's threatening. But the truth is that we are all self-made, even if only the successful will admit it. Once you accept absolute responsibility, you'll immediately begin improving. You'll eliminate excuses. You'll decide what kind of experiences you want to have and you'll become accountable to yourself. You'll also find yourself becoming more persistent, more courageous, and more determined.

Does accepting total responsibility make sense to you? It did to Nobel Prize winner, George Bernard Shaw. Shaw said, "People are always blaming their circumstances for what they are. I don't believe in circumstances. The people who get on in this world are the people who get up and look for the circumstances they want and if they can't find them, they make them."

Chinese Bamboo Plant by Joel Weldon, "The Weldon Blueprint"

Remember, ideas are valuable only when you act on them. Action will be the difference between just dreaming about a better you and building a better you. Finally, if your progress seems too slow. If you feel you're not accelerating as fast as you'd like to, remember the Moso, a Chinese bamboo plant. When a farmer plants a Moso, he can take care of it for an entire year. Watering, weeding, and fertilizing, but not see any signs of growth, not so much as a tiny sprout. He can continue pampering his Moso for another full year and still not see any signs of growth. It can go on like this for up to five years. By then, you'd think that any farmer would give up. But suddenly, five years after it was planted, the Moso will nose its way through the soil, and within just six weeks, it will become a towering, 90-foot high, Chinese bamboo plant. Ninety feet! That's the height of a 9-story office building, all in just six weeks!

How is that possible? Well, all those years when the farmer saw no growth above the ground, the Moso was spreading its root system, miles of roots, getting ready. And that's what you might need to do before you achieve the results you desire. So have patience. It could take you a while to spread your roots and clear your thinking of the fears and doubts that previously held you back. But when you do, you will progress as suddenly and as visibly as the Moso does. Your potential is amazing and it's just begging to be released. Begin tapping that potential today, so you can continue building a better you!

Visualize again that towering Chinese bamboo plant, the Moso. See those thick shoots. They are able to withstand fierce winds. And after growing ninety feet within six weeks, the

Moso can continue thriving for a long time. But when does it die? Would you consider it dead only after it crashes to the ground, all brown and withered? Well it could be. But, I believe the Moso, just like a human being, begins dying as soon as it stops growing.

The single essential sign of life is growth. When the Moso stops growing, it's dying. When you and I stop growing, we're dying. We may appear to be alive. We may continue breathing walking and talking, but if we're not growing as a person, we are dying. It all comes down to one simple statement: "When you're green you grow. When you're ripe you rot." As good as you are now, you can be even better. Do you believe that? Are you committed to tapping your potential?

Dendrocalamus giganteus (*Graminaea*): Bamboo, the largest known grass, 90-120 feet high with diameters from 10-12 inches and 16-18 inches between the joints. There are five genera and 280 species. (Malaya, Ceylon, and Burma)

Modern Day Mountain Man

Utah's own entrepreneur extraordinaire, Dick Bass, has been responsible for bringing many visitors to Utah and introducing them to his dreams. Living life to the fullest, he is a man of adventure and states in his book, *The Seven Peaks*, "A good adventure needs to combine some risk-taking, some unvisited, untracked, or unexplored territory, and some physical challenge."

When I first met Mr. Bass over twelve years ago on a plane trip, he was wearing a neck brace, which didn't slow him down from enthusiastically sharing his philosophy and passion to develop "body, mind and spirit." He continuously coaxed me to come up to visit his ski resort called Snowbird where "the powder snow is waist deep. There's no place in the world like the Bird. Come and ski me!" Then with a big grin he admitted that he couldn't stop talking about the things he loved. "They call me the 'Big Mouth Bass' he laughed.

This wonderful man shared some of his life's adventures, which included his quest to climb the seven highest mountains on each continent, including Mt. Everest. He got married on top of the Matterhorn. He swam the Dardanelle's, a 2-and-a-half-mile swim across Hellespont in Turkey, and then jogged the 31 miles over the original route that the ancient Greek runner Philippides ran when he carried the marathon victory message into Athens.

Dick feels that he always does his best when he has a challenge right in front of him to focus on. He has developed an optimism that gives him the ability to smile in the face of adversity. He has faith that through hard work and smart work everything will be just fine. He tenaciously eliminates defeatist thoughts from his mind and quotes his uncle as having taught him as a boy, "Just remember, men are made strong not by winning easy battles, but by losing hard-fought ones."

Mr. Bass is no stranger to disappointment and defeat. After returning to safety from danger he reflects, "you are left with a vague yearning, a kind of strange addiction, cousin to whatever it is that lures men and women to take physical risk of their lives." However, even in defeat he is positive and often quotes Falstaff: "He who fights and runs away, lives to fight another day, but he who in the battle is slain, will never rise to fight again."

His attitude is that "obstacles are merely things to overcome." We often "start projects motivated by achieving things that could be measured objectively, but learned that the real goal was to achieve subjective things or intangibles that couldn't be measured finitely at all."

This 'modern day mountain man' has started at the bottom of many of life's mountains. He has climbed to the top and has survived the elements. His life's message resonates with the need to deal with unexpected demands and interruptions. His self-confidence comes by enjoying life as an adventure, setting fantastic goals, and never giving up!

Balance

We need a whole-life philosophy and process implemented with systems providing us with everything we need to increase our productivity, find and preserve peace and happiness and a healthy balance in life to be able to magnify ourselves and our spheres of influence. . We must learn how to expand our horizons and be more effective in our efforts through learned principles and dynamic skill development.

We will learn that we do not have to be successful or wealthy to be happy, but we do have to give our best efforts. We must learn to achieve inner peace and balance in life and reduce unexpected demands and interruptions on our time. We need to use the correct principles and skills to identify our highest priorities, set and achieve meaningful goals, and reduce stress. We must identify and control our "time robbers" including procrastination and interruptions.

As we pull together and focus on the things that matter most, we will find the resources to accomplish our goals. We can do it if we believe we can and if we do it together.

"Buried here are all the ideas never invented . . .all the great products never made . . . all the best sellers never written . . . masterpieces never painted . . . innovations never completed . . . dreams never fulfilled."

    - Anonymous

Chapter 7

Excellence and Quality

"Revolution means turning the wheel."
- Igor Stravinsky

I Love New York

My wife and I had the opportunity to serve a church mission in New York City. I love New York and especially living in Harlem. Every day, I felt that it was my full-time job to say hello to everyone and smile at them. Wishing others a good day lifted my spirits at the same time. I always tried to be prepared with some quarters, dimes, nickels or pennies to give to beggars on the street. Occasionally, I had to keep some back to give to another friend on the next corner.

My favorite greeting to younger children was to ask if they obeyed their parents. I talked to many hundreds of children. They would usually look to Mom and Dad for approval to answer. I had the parents' ear and even the attention of many others on the bus, train, or sidewalk. Then I would say, "If you obey your mother (or father), you will always be happy. That's my promise! If you don't obey, I can't promise you happiness." The children usually nodded their head affirmatively or began telling me what a good boy or girl they were. The parents almost always gave me a smile a big silent, "Thank you!" as we moved along.

With older children and teenagers with backpacks, sports gear, or cell phones, I'd ask if they were a good student or good at what it looked like they were going to do. I mostly got, "Yeah, I'm pretty good." Then I'd say, "Don't just be good, be great! You can be great. The difference is in how you think and how you feel in your heart."

Now, away from New York, at the end of the day and at the beginning of each new day I have an opportunity to dust away negative thoughts from my mind and wash away the bad things in my heart. I'm grateful to be alive! I'm glad I can make a difference.

Set Measurable Standards of Excellence

In old English common law, the "Rule of Thumb" was that you could not beat your wife with a stick any bigger than your thumb. We have come a long way and now use this phase, "rule of thumb," to mean a good measurement of something. There are thousands of factors contributing to greatness and to success or failure. However, there are some practices, attitudes, and characteristics that will help indicate whether or not a particular path is worth following or an opportunity is worth pursuing. Remember, "Practice makes permanent."

Life is a progressive process of learning who we are and discovering what we can become. You can come to understand and measure what challenges attract you and foster greatness in you. You can decide what motivates you, satisfies your curiosity and stimulates your intellect and desire. What are your expectations of yourself? What resources do you want to work with? How do you want to be recognized and rewarded? Do you want a coach, a friend, or mentor to encourage your personal development? What makes you feel important, and who do you like to be around? Are opportunities to learn and grow important? These questions are like tickets to the ball park. They can get you into the game, but they can't help you win.

It's important to know the answers to these questions and to have a way to measure how you are doing in relationship to them. If you feel you are not totally engaged in your family, work, or personal development, it's your responsibility to ask questions and determine for yourself what is working and what isn't. The answers are the fuel to your future. If you are not engaged or are meandering around, then you are losing your life's fuel.

Focus on results by:

1. helping others establishing meaningful long and short-term goals
2. help them take personal responsibility
3. provide feedback
4. champion their creativity and initiatives; an
5. operate with speed and intensity.

Help them bring ideas to action and push for the next step with energy, enthusiasm and urgency. Help them always look for ways to improve as you do the same.

It's important to generate action and results, not just motion. Don't just please others. Decide which actions must stop, which should start and which should continue. Actions must be:

1. result oriented
2. realistic
3. recognizable
4. real-time to do today.

Keep track of your own performance and learning. In a work environment, this reduces the tendency for you to use self-assessment as a negotiating tool. Share the whole record of successes, failures and perceived strengths etc. The point is self-discovery.

Enjoy Others

Great people love their friends and families. They love their work. They receive great satisfaction in helping others succeed. In climbing any mountain, you have to climb it in stages: What do I get? What do I give? Do I belong here? How can we all grow? If you can answer positively to all these questions, then you have reached the summit.

It is not easy to stay on the summit for long. The ground is shifting, and the winds are blowing. The key is to build a strong, vibrant environment at Base Camp and Camp 1. It is important to focus on the basics first before aiming too high and too fast. Don't helicopter in at 17,000 feet, because sooner or later you and others may die on the mountain. Set consistent expectations for everyone.

Care about each person, praise each person, and if necessary, sometimes distance yourself from a person you have cared about and praised. Great people balance their lives by being around the right people.

Capitalize on people's differences and help them become more and more of who they already are. People don't change that much. Don't waste time trying to put in what was left out. Try to draw out what was left in. That is hard enough.

Develop your own checklist to help you progress and keep balanced. Like an airplane pilot, you can and should evaluate before and after every flight. It will help you prevent crashes, excess costs, and time wasted. For a happy balanced life, my friend Lynn Robbins recommends the following:

Recipe for Success

1. Be passionate. Love what you do.
2. The greatest wealth is family and friends. Enjoy their love.
3. Make every day the best it can be.
4. "No" is unacceptable. Don't stop there. Go for "yes."
5. Celebrate and measure excellence. Feel important and help make other people feel important.
6. The GREATEST FAILURE is not to try.

Mix with:

> Philosophy of Excellence: Good enough never is.
> Attitude of excellence: When things are bad, it means that good is close by.
> Report card of excellence: Get wows!
> Bake it for about 20 years - and voilà!

Your peak performance has absolutely nothing to do with others' expectations and measurements. It has everything to do with your expectations and measurements. You can create your own scorecards. There are a few tools that help us measure our progress along the way. There are many others to consider, but the basics include:

1. a personal resume and biographical sketch
2. a personal financial statement
3. your personal life plan.

You can choose your own resume form, but always put your strengths first. Your biographical sketch should highlight your passions and your strongest achievements. Most people only fill out a personal financial statement when we apply for a loan to purchase a house or car. All our married life of forty years, we have used our own financial statement. I soon tired of filling the bank form out, and created my own on an Excel spreadsheet. I've shared the form with hundreds of family and friends and always give it to newlyweds along with other financial advice. We update ours regularly, at least annually and sometimes more often as needed.

It will become your personal scorecard showing you the progress of developing your net worth. It keeps you on track and can be a great motivator. I recommend you develop your own ASAP. Your life plan will consist of your mission statement, governing values, lifetime goals, five or 10 year goals and then yearly goals. With this, you can use your daily planning tool to accomplish monthly, weekly and daily tasks in achieving lifetime goals, living your values and being your mission statement.

If you don't have your life plan developed – do it! Do it right! And do it right now! If you do this, I promise you that great things will happen in your life because you will discover the greatness within and that will result in you doing great things. When you do great things, great things will also happen in your life.

These are valuable and indispensable tools in knowing where you've been, where you are, and where you are going. You need to understand the purpose of these score cards. You must understand how to use them for your own personal development and for working with others.

Develop a system and routine that provides frequent personal introspection, measurement, and evaluation. You must do it more than once or twice a year. Frequent performance evaluation will force you to pay attention and make needed changes. You will avoid the big battles by having small skirmishes. Focusing on the future requires a discussion of what "could be."

Parable of the Unwise Manager

A certain business owner went out of state and purchased another company. Before he left town after the acquisition, he called his staff of ten new managers and gave them their new responsibilities, assignments, and duties. He also appointed to each new manager one assistant. He said unto them, "Carry on until I return."

But his employees under the managers hated him and did not accept well this change in management. They sent letters and e-mails saying, "We don't like the changes you've made with the managers you have placed over us.

And it came to pass, that when he was returned, having completed the acquisition and merger, he commanded the managers to be called unto him, that he might know how much every man had filled his assignments and responsibilities.

Then came the first, saying, "Boss, I have leveraged my efforts working with one employee and have generated enough business to keep ten employees busy." And the owner said unto him, "Well, thou good manager. Because thou hast been successful in a very little, I will hire nine more employees so you can manage ten employees."

The second came in, saying, "Boss, I have leveraged my efforts working with one employee and have generated enough business to keep five employees busy." And the owner said likewise unto him, "I will hire four more employees for you to manage."

And another came, saying," Boss, behold, here is my one employee, which I have kept busy doing all the things I didn't have time to do. Business has not been so good, but we have enough business to pay for our salary and expenses. I was afraid of you, because you're a shrewd businessman. You seem to generate business without much effort and where it seems impossible to succeed."

The owner said to him, "I will decide what to do with you, you unwise manager. You knew I was a shrewd businessman and succeed with little effort. For that reason, I gave you an opportunity to succeed by having an employee to help leverage your efforts so when I asked for an accounting, you would show me a profit."

And he said unto them that stood by, "Take from him the one employee, and give that employee to him that hath ten employees." And they said unto him, "Boss, he already has ten employees." The boss explained that he wanted to focus his resources on the most successful managers and get rid of those who were not producing. He brought in the other unsuccessful managers and fired them on the spot.

Now, here I've done it again. I've used a parable describing a business example. You may be asking yourself, "How do I apply this to my personal, family or community life?" I believe that this is the beauty of any parable. If you read to understand the principles that it teaches, you will quickly and almost seamlessly be able to apply it as needed or as you desire. My challenge to you is to sit down with a pen and piece of paper consider your life or others in your family or community. Think of how you or someone else is not living up to the potential or greatness within. Think about related desires, goals or ambitions and the fear that holds one back. You do the math and write your own parable. You be the teacher or teller and share what you have learned and life or be lifted. I know you have it within you. You can do it.

Parable of the Lost Unit of Inventory

What supply manager, having ten units of inventory, having lost one, wouldn't search the warehouse and delivery trucks until it's found? And when it's found, the manager will pull his team into his office and say, "Let's party, I found the lost inventory!" You can bet your booties, there is rejoicing in the board room when lost inventory is found.

Performance Planning Meetings

Try these ideas the next time you feel a need to be motivated to organize your closet and stuff or sit the family down and give everyone their chores. Perhaps you are helping with a PTA function or community clean up project. Whatever it is, planning meetings are vital to great success.

Be future oriented. Have participants prepare by writing down answers to:

1. What *actions* have you taken?
2. What *discoveries* have you made?
3. What *partnerships* have you built?
4. What is your *main focus*?

This will help you, as a guide set appropriate expectations and know how to run interference for the employee. This approach will help you be a stronger partner by meeting more frequently, listening, paying attention, advising, planning in detail, and developing a shared and realistic interest in the participants' success. And the employee will have a record of it.

An employee needs to become increasingly clear about his or her skills, knowledge, and talents. He need to understand, in detail, what the next steps are. Managers can help by asking these five career discovery questions:

1. How do you describe success in your current role? Add your own thoughts by saying, "This is what I think. . . . "
2. What do you do that makes you feel good, and what does this tell you about you skills, knowledge, and talents? Add your own thoughts by saying, "This is what I think. . . ."
3. What part of your current role do you enjoy the most and why?
4. What part do you struggle with, and what does this tell you about your skills, knowledge and talents? How can we manage around this?
5. What would be the perfect role for you, and why? Add your own thoughts by saying, "This is what I think. . . ."

No guide or manager can make an employee productive. They are catalysts, however, who can help an employee find his path of least resistance and plan his career to be a superstar. A manager is an agent, helping employees to look at themselves, evaluate and keep track of their progress, discover themselves, build relationships, and catch their peers doing something right.

Work with Your Guide

If you are an participant, and your guide or manager is too busy to talk, then schedule a meeting (at least every 3 months) and let them know you will provide the structure. If your guide or manager forces you to do things his way, let him know you want to define your role more by what to outcome than merely by steps you should take. This will not only help them clarify what needs to be done, but how, when and why. You may need to explain that your approach is different and a more efficient way for you to reach the desired outcomes.

If your manager praises you inappropriately, pick your moments to explain what would best motive you. If your manager constantly asks you questions about how you are doing or feeling or otherwise intrudes, ask if you could check in less frequently and explain that you would like to be a little more independent. If your manager ignores, disrespects, or distrusts you, takes credit for your work, or blames you for mistakes, get out from under him. Don't fool yourself. If his behavior has been consistent over time, he is not going to change that much. Some managers simply should not be managers.

Fox and the Hedgehog

> *"The fox knows many things, but the hedgehog knows one big thing."*
> - Isaiah Berllin

Foxes are known to be fast and clever and masters of escape. Hedgehogs are known to be slow, methodical and focused. They are not stupid. Authors have described the essence of this profound insight as *simplicity*. Hedgehogs see what is essential, and ignore the rest. The world is overrun by management faddists, brilliant visionaries, ranting futurists, fear mongers, motivational gurus, and all the rest. It's great to see a person or an organization take one simple concept and just do it with excellence and imagination.

Three circles of the hedgehog concept:

1. What are you deeply passionate about?
2. What can you be the best at?
3. What drives your emotional, social and economic engine?

The Hedgehog Concept is not a goal, strategy, or intention; it is an understanding of what you can be the best at. Stick with what you understand and let your abilities, not your ego, determine what you attempt.

This requires a severe standard of excellence. It's not about building a strength or competence, but about understanding what an individual's or an organization's potential is in being the very best.

Make a Difference by Stretching and Reaching Beyond Expectations

Good is the enemy of excellence. Greatness is the challenge to be something more than average. Jim Rohn says that great leaders produce great results, good leaders tend to produce good results and poor leaders have an adverse impact.

Turnover

Great leaders have a desire to make things happen with and for other people. Poor leaders have a desire to make things happen for themselves. Turnover costs companies millions of dollars every year. The relationship an employee has with his or her manager substantially influences the employee's decision to stay with a company or move on.

There is a human tendency to blame problems on low performers. Pogo said, "We have met the enemy and he is us." People often confuse personality traits with leadership. Discipline is always more important than some natural ability. Without discipline and willingness to learn, those with natural ability will never progress above their current skill level.

Prodigies show a pattern of interest in their talents. They practice from between two to six or more hours a day for many years. Progress stops when they switch to just playing and stop practicing.

Focus More on Quality than Quantity

Take the best and leave the rest. Focus on results by developing the gardener as well as producing the fruit. If you focus on the work and not the fruit, it will only be work. If you focus on work and the fruit, there will be success with both the gardener and the crop.

Define Success and Failure

Insanity is defined as continuing to do the same thing, but expecting different results.

Define success as achieving what you want while enjoying what you have. Success is what you want it to be. Success is the appropriate action and use of knowledge, skills, and resources to achieve a desired result. Success can be good or bad, depending on the desired result and the means to achieve it. Success means different things to different people. You need to determine what success means to you.

The preface to the book, *Born To Win*, by Lewis Timberlake, says, "I don't understand . . . how a black cow can eat green grass which turns into white milk and yellow butter . . . how a caterpillar encases itself in its homemade casket and changes into a beautiful butterfly; how its hair changes into scales (one million to a square inch); how its many legs become the six legs of the butterfly; and how its yellow color turns into a brilliant red . . . how a handful of sand deposited in the heart of the earth is miraculously changed into a fiery opal when heat is applied from beneath and ponderous weight from above . . . how a handful of black carbon planted deep in the bowels of the earth is transformed into a glorious diamond when that same heat and weight are applied . . . how oxygen and hydrogen (both of them odorless, tasteless, and colorless) can combine with black, insoluble, tasteless carbon to become sweet, white sugar . . . how the human heart, only 6 inches in length and 4 inches in diameter, can beat seventy times per minute, 4,200 times per hour, 100,800 times per day, 36,792,000 times per year, and 2,575,440,000 times in an average lifetime . . . how that same tiny heart could be so successful that, every time it beats, it pumps blood at a rate of 2.5 ounces per beat, 175 ounces per minute, 656 pounds per hour, and 7.75 tons per day! . . . why some people are born with so little and yet achieve so much . . . why some who have so much seem to accomplish so very little."

He continues by saying, "Although I am only one out of a million, I am somebody, and that makes me as good as the next man. There is nothing in this life I cannot do. There is no goal I cannot tackle and have success! If I feel deep down inside that something is important to me, then I can do it. If my mind can conceive it and my head can believe it then I know I can achieve it. No longer will I drift through life feeling sorry for myself, because self-pity is the seed of destruction. I will search for a goal, and with enough hard work, total commitment, determination, dedication, and self-sacrifice, I know I will reach it. I know there will be many times when it will seem that all the odds are against me, and I will have to fight one battle after another -- but I will not give up!"

Success is being great!

"Success is peace of mind which is a direct result of self-satisfaction in knowing you did your best to become the best you are capable of becoming."
- John Wooden

"If you want a place in the sun, you must expect some blisters."
- Anonymous

"If you think training is expensive, try ignorance."
- Anonymous

Success is often measured in knowledge, wealth and prosperity, power, friendship or relationships, posterity and liberty. But in reality, success is each man finding the work he can do best, doing it to his highest satisfaction, and getting proof of his service in a suitable reward.

If he is the kind of man who has still greater visions of service he will get enough money to fulfill his service. There is no harm in having large sums of money if it is kept to work opening up lines of opportunity and service. The only harmful money is the money that lies idle or is used to block progress.

In every success, whether it be personal or industrial, the same qualities are necessary. These cannot be imitated. They must be the real thing. They must live in the individual and grow out of their nature. They must be developed, trained, and kept under discipline. No man wins success without paying for it. No person fails without good reason.

Law of Success and Law of Failure

The law of success is no respecter of persons. If a good man is a failure it is because he has failed to fulfill the law of success. There is no favoritism. The law of success is a fair law. It gives all a chance. It does not choose the extraordinary and favor him. Successful people are just ordinary people, who have applied themselves to one thing and paid the price to win.

The law of failure is just as fair. Honest people fail and disrespectful people fail. Hard-hearted people fail and kind human beings fail. Why? To find the reason we must examine failure as carefully as we examine success. There is always a good reason.

There is no success without application. This means concentration of mind, labor of hand and brain, and a complete surrender of one's own plan.

There must be courage. Unless you have tried to do something for yourself you have no idea how often your courage will be tested or how often you will stare failure fully in the face. You will have no idea how many almost crushing obstacles will arise to fall on you and block the way.

Success then is a matter of certain qualities coming into play. But you cannot imitate a quality. You must create it, develop it.

If you are fooled into thinking that hardness and dishonesty are qualities of success, you will find yourself mistaken. You must develop the right characteristics if you would be successful.

You Can Make a Difference!

"That man is a success who has lived well, laughed often, and loved much; who has gained the respect of intelligent men and the love of children; who has filled his niche and accomplished his task; who leaves the world better than he found it, whether by an improved poppy, a perfect poem, or a rescued soul; who never lacked appreciation of earth's beauty or failed to express it; who looked for the best in others and gave the best he had."

- Robert Louis Stevenson

"Not often in the story of mankind does a man arrive on earth who is both steel and velvet, who is as hard as rock and soft as drifting fog, who holds in his heart and mind the paradox of terrible storm and peace unspeakable and perfect."

- Carl Sandburg, on 150th anniversary of Abraham Lincoln's birth.

"Recipe For Greatness: To bear up under loss; To fight the bitterness of defeat and the weakness of grief; To be victor over anger; To smile when tears are close; To resist disease and evil men and base instincts; To reject hate and to encourage love; To go on when it would seem good to die; To look up with unquenchable faith in something ever more about to be. That is what any man can do, and be great."

- Zane Gray

Continuously improvement

Training never ends. We learn to do by doing. It has been said that practice makes perfect, but actually practice makes permanent. Practice doesn't make perfect, but perfect practice makes perfect.

Start immediately to motivate yourself. Apply your own incentives. Remember the costs, and focus on the reward.

The real competition is with self. From small things come great things. You need to decide if you are going to work for someone or work for yourself. Change your life by turning ideas into habits. Watch for cues and recognize the call to action. Rehearse with a friend and get honest feedback.

Leadership Change

We lead by example. Leaders cast a significant shadow in the organization where they work. This shadow can cut both ways. If you work with an extraordinary or great leader, the tendency is that your leadership effectiveness will be close to your own leaders. On the other hand, if your boss is not an effective leader, the tendency is that you won't be much better. The length of time people spend with the same boss can increase the size of the shadow. Some have a 100 percent overlap.

The process mimicking the strengths and weaknesses of one's boss is an unconscious process. Child abuse is an example. Children who are abused have a high likelihood of becoming abusive parents. Employees are rarely more effective than their bosses. Bosses set the standards, high or low. Some bosses encourage subordinates to be their clones and reinforce their own behaviors. The best way to bring about real change is to change the leaders.

Learn from Mistakes and Adjust

Feedback works. Great people welcome negative feedback. People are either "improving" or "proving". Those improving view the world as an opportunity to learn and grow. The proving group sees life as a process of justifying or proving themselves to others.

Assess areas of strengths and weakness. There are some weaknesses called fatal flaws that lead to failure. Don't dwell on weaknesses, but you must fix your fatal flaws. These include the inability to learn from mistakes, lack of interpersonal skills, lack of open mindedness, lack of accountability, and lack of initiative. If you don't fix these, you'll never be great, and you may do a lot of harm.

There is a ripple effect from these flaws, and everyone feels their impact. Some people say, "Don't rock the boat." Two people may respond very differently to exactly the same feedback, based on their life orientation. One may say, "Don't touch a project that might fail." "It doesn't matter whether you win or lose; it's how you place the blame." With these people, the key is to do as little as possible and survive. Keep your head down. Don't draw attention. Such smothered employees become incapable of taking initiative or embracing new ideas. Some never recover. Don't be like this!

Improve Faster than Changes

No technology, no matter how great, can by itself ignite a shift from good to great. Avoid technology fads and bandwagons, but become a pioneer in the application of carefully selected technologies. The key question about any technology is, "Does the technology fit directly with your

ENERGY

passion?" If yes, then you need to become a pioneer in the application of that technology. If no, then you can settle for something similar or ignore it entirely. Don't let yourself be motivated by the fear of being left behind.

Monitor, Measure, and Analyze

In business leadership roles and industry advancement, performance and progress are measures of greatness. They are:

1. High productivity
2. Low turnover
3. High customer satisfaction
4. High profitability
5. Innovation
6. Positive relationship with suppliers.

These same indicators can be applied to our individual personal lives.

Effective leadership is best defined and measured by the *results* produced. Greatness is first measured by *personal* and *group fulfillment* and then by results.

Some managers think their job is to put the pressure on to get desired results. To do this, they must separate the excellent performers from the average ones, and the average ones from the poor ones. Typical performance review systems encourage us to sort people into top, average, and poor performers – regardless of where they really fit. It also sets people up to compete with each other. It eliminates cooperation and team spirit.

Managers should be asked at evaluation time, "Shall we go out and hire some losers so we can fill some of our low slots? No, you either hire winners or potential winners. If you don't *hire* people on a performance review curve, why grade them on one? Greatness implies that everyone has the opportunity to win. It will encourage people to compete against themselves and not against each other. Don't punish someone who is not able to perform up to standard. Instead, help her to find a position where she can succeed.

Continuous monitoring, frequent feedback, measuring and analyzing are far better than annual evaluations. This forces everyone to pay attention, and it makes it so much easier to address problems or poor performance. This avoids the battle of wills by having small skirmishes.

Bully or Build

When leaders (team captains, parents, older siblings or supervisors) attempt to improve their focus on results, they often put a great deal of emphasis on the drive or push to emphasize results. When done in excess, such leaders become grown-up bullies who constantly prod, check, demand, and annoy others. These behaviors can be effective in the short run, but in the long run, nobody wants to work for a bully.

Strength Interview

In a strength interview you can ask: What do you enjoy most? What brought you hear? What keeps you here? What are your strengths and weaknesses? What are your goals, scores, and timelines? How often do you like to meet? What is the best praise you have received, and what made it so good? Have you had real productive partnerships or mentors, and why did these relationships work so well for you? What are your growth, skill, and career goals, and how can I help? Is there anything else you want to talk about that would help us work together?

Focus on the 20/80 Rule

Focus on the 20 percent effort that gives 80 percent of the results. Greatness comes from a cumulative process—step by step, action by action, decision by decision. The right people want to be part of a winning team. They want to contribute to producing visible, tangible results. They want to feel the excitement of being involved in something that just flat-out works. Greatness doesn't happen in a moment, but is the fruit of seeds planted, nourished, and pruned over a long period time.

Don't allow success or achievements to dominate your life. Success and achievement become like blood and water to a healthy body. They are absolutely essential for life, but they are not the purpose of life. Preserve your values and purpose while your strategies and operating practices endlessly adapt to a changing world. Greatness doesn't depend on size.

If we focused on the most important things and ignored the rest, our lives would be much simpler and our results vastly improved. We run best at the end when it counts the most. Running is fun. If you're not passionate about what you do, then go find something else to do. Focus on the right things, not the wrong things.

Chapter 8

Think Strategically

"Make lemonade from lemons!"
- Anonymous

"The roses of success rise from the ashes of defeat."
- Movie Chiti Chiti Bang Bang

Approach Things Strategically

As important as goal setting is, defining, planning, and implementing your methods and actions is just as important. This is what strategy is all about. In a business setting, the planning and process of hiring and utilizing human resources is called *strategy*. The methods and execution or implementation are called *tactics*.

Recognize the purpose behind your strategy. Sometimes we confuse wants with strategy. A business manager must ask other employees or we must ask ourselves, "Why do you want that?" Before you can agree on a congruent purpose, you must know what the real purposes are. Separate what they are demanding from the purpose it serves. Invent a mutual purpose. By focusing on higher and longer-term goals we can transcend short-term compromises. Brainstorm new strategies by actively coming up with options that can serve everyone. Don't aim for perfection, aim for progress.

Synergy

Synergy is defined as the cooperative action of (different parts) such that the total effect is greater than the sum of the effects taken independently. Synergos (Greek) means working together. Common goals create synergism. For example, if one 2" x 4" board two feet long can support 600 pounds, then it would stand to reason that two similar boards would support 1,200 pounds. In actuality, two such boards can support 2,000 pounds. That's synergism!

Anticipate Your Next Move and Adapt to Change

Maintaining "stress fitness" through appropriate mental exercise, physical activity, and social exchange. Physical, mental, and emotional health fitness is vital our success in achieving our potential. It is a law of nature that we need opposition in all things. Perception and attitude determines whether this opposition is positive or negative.

Life itself is an education. We are mental, emotional, and spiritual beings having a physical experience. We all are born, grow to puberty, then maturity until death. Sickness and stress is all a process of evolving and growing. Belief, change for better, commitment, and following your heart are all common in the language of religions and philosophers throughout the ages.

In the popular movie, *The Lion King*, Elton John shares the beautiful words to the song "Circle of Life":

> *From the day we arrive on the planet*
> *And blinking, step into the sun*
> *There's more to see than can ever be seen*
> *More to do than can ever be done*

There's far too much to take in here
  More to find than can ever be found
But the sun rolling high/Through the sapphire sky
  Keeps great and small on the endless round

Some say eat or be eaten
  Some say live and let live
But all are agreed as they join the stampede
  You should never take more than you give

Some of us fall by the wayside
  And some of us soar to the stars
And some of us sail through our troubles
  And some have to live with the scars

It's the circle of life and it moves us all
  Through despair and hope
Through faith and love
  Till we find our place on the path unwinding

In the circle of life, in the circle of life.

Climbing Mountains

Cuzco Yacta is the Qechua name for the magnificent city of Cuzco located high in the *aliplano* among the Andes Mountains of Peru. Literally translated, this name means "the umbilical cord of the world" or "where all life began." Ancient Indian legends describe the creation, the flood, and a visit by the white-bearded God named Viracocha. Peru was the birthplace of ancient civilizations and is a sacred part of this land.

It is not uncommon for foreign tourists, as well as Peruvians living at lower altitudes, to get altitude sickness (*Saroche*) when they first arrive. It takes some rest time for the body to adjust. The locals offer coca tea to speed up the process. I lived with my family in Peru for three years. My physical reactions were different each time during my many visits high in the Andes Mountains. Most generally, I had a slight headache and or mild nausea. Some people became very ill. Others pass out unless they take the time to adjust before going further. There is a lesson in greatness to be learned from this.

It is not easy to climb high mountains. The higher the altitude the less oxygen we get with each breath. Our bodies need to adapt or we get weak and sick. The beauty of our body is that it can and will adapt if we give let it. The same applies for our mind and spirit. As we rise to higher altitudes of nobler causes or loftier thoughts, we can adapt and continue on to do great things. In the doing, we inspire others to follow and do the same. Each of us has our limits and levels of tolerance, but we can adapt and move on to greater heights.

Know What You Want and How to Get It

Greatness is fueled by creativity, imagination, bold moves into uncharted waters, and visionary zeal. The purpose of family traditions, business policy or government bureaucracy is to compensate for incompetence and lack of discipline. Avoid bureaucracy and hierarchy and instead create a culture of discipline. When you are disciplined and work with disciplined people, you don't need hierarchy, bureaucracy, or excessive controls. When you combine a culture of discipline with creativity and a strong work ethic, you get the magical alchemy of greatness, performance and sustained results.

Disciplined action without self-disciplined people is impossible to sustain. Disciplined action without disciplined thought is a recipe for disaster. Well-meaning tyrants are leaders who get things done by sheer force and personality and create a culture of discipline that will not endure. People will be frozen by indecision and inability to do anything. You never want to be this kind of leader.

Accomplishment in Relationship to Objectives

Change your plans, but never what you measure yourself against. Never just focus on what you accomplished, but what you accomplished relative to what you said you were going to accomplish – no matter how tough the measure. This is responsible accounting.

Bureaucratic cultures arise to compensate for incompetence and lack of discipline, which arise from having the wrong people in public office in the first place. A culture of discipline is not just about action. It is about getting disciplined people who engage in disciplined thought and who then take disciplined action. Do not confuse a culture of discipline with a tyrant. The challenge becomes, not opportunity creation, but opportunity selection.

The fact that something is a "once-in-a lifetime opportunity" is irrelevant unless it helps you achieve your goals. The "stop doing" lists are sometimes more important than "to do" lists. Once you know the right things, you must have the discipline to do the right thing and to stop doing the wrong things.

Do the Right Things

Do the right things rather than just do things right. Identify and clarify what you really want to do and to be and stay focused no matter what happens. You can change their own heart, but it will require effort and discipline. Most of us are quick to blame others and don't see what we contribute the problems we're experiencing. Great people start with themselves and continually try to improve.

Search for more creative and productive options. Don't make unwise choices like either/or choices between two bad options. Locate your own "North Star" and take charge. In relationships with others, wanting to win drives us away from healthy dialogue. Seeking revenge causes us to move from wanting to win to wanting to harm the other person. Hoping to remain safe often causes us to go silent. We seek peace over conflict.

Good people do things right. Great people do the right things. The difference is one of focus. Good people look from the outside inward. Great people look from the inside outward. Great people are not waiting for opportunities to be thrust upon them. They are working to create opportunities. They have not just developed sophistication and smoothness, they are developing success.

Calculate and Manage Risk

Be a risk taker. As a person of greatness, a leader or business owner, entrust resources, responsibility and authority with those who have the most ability and character. This means investing in yourself. If you are a leader or business owner, it means investing in new procedures, new products, new markets, and new people. It means taking prudent risks.

Prepare for Tough Times

The Boy Scout motto, "Be Prepared" applies to individuals as well as organizations. Prosperity will grow out of poverty, but that prosperity can evaporate very quickly. We must have a sure foundation before building the grand and beautiful. Individually, we should have a supply of food, fuel, clothing and money for emergencies. Businesses that are high-flying front-runners without reserves and without a plan for the tough times do not survive. Personally and in business, we must prepare for both the general tough times and the specific periods of crisis that are likely to come. All economies are cyclical. There will be downturns, recessions, and maybe even depressions. Financial reserves and an orderly plan for tightening our built or for downsizing a company during these times are often keys to survival. Too, there are likely to be times of crisis specific to your personal situation and/or business. Both a crisis plan and a general damage-control plan need to be in place.

An entire chapter could be dedicated to this topic. However, such a chapter is not the intent of this book. The above paragraph is intended to be a warning that will be recognized by people of greatness and shared with those of lesser character. Let those that see, hear and understand seek out the necessary information to put into practice the principles mentioned. Doing so is an attribute of greatness.

Timing Is Important

Punctuality is the courtesy of the kings. If we are late we send messages to others that they are not important. We are saying that my time is more important than your time. This is an arrogant message. We also send the message that we do not stick to our word or keep our commitments.

There is a profound poem etched in the metal of a sundial located on the campus of Wellesley College just west of Boston. It reads:

> *The shadow by my finger cast,*
> *Divides the future from the past.*
> *Behind its unreturning line*
> *the vanished hour, no longer thine.*
> *Before it lies the unknown hour,*
> *In darkness and beyond thy power.*
> *One hour alone is in thine hands,*
> *The now on which the shadow stands.*

Timing should always be a consideration in your personal life and in family or business planning. Whether it's a graduation, wedding announcement or birth of a baby, major announcements should be timed for maximum impact. Such events, efforts and products should be introduced at the most opportune time. Where appropriate, they can be planned around significant anniversaries and public holidays. Timing should also be a consideration in releasing the inevitable bad news that every person, family or organization has from time to time.

In any event or whether personal or public, be responsive and take care of business on the spot. Return calls and answer correspondence. Don't just put things on hold unless there is a strategic reason for doing so.

Meetings Management

A meeting (one-on-one, family, church, civic business or volunteer) is the process of conducting a productive, effective, and purposeful gathering. It is a process of people instructing, motivating one another and sharing information while participating in a decision making process. Before giving any examples, let me mention that the principles described here are applicable to personal and family meetings. In every case except when you have a private meeting with yourself, there is another person or other people involved. The numbers of people and the costs will vary, but the process is the same and the principles are equally applicable.

A meeting can be a great tool, but they are very costly. For example, let's calculate the cost of a three-hour meeting for ten people. If their average salary was $60,000 per year, that's $5,000 per month, $1,250 per week or $21 per hour in a forty-hour work week. A one- hour meeting costs $630.

There are many different types of meetings. The format of the meeting, and how it is conducted, makes a big difference on how effective a meeting can be. Remember to ask:

1. WHAT type of meeting is needed
2. HOW the meeting should be conducted

There are several formats for meetings, including:

1. One-on-One (planned or spontaneous)
2. Informal (small or large)
3. Formal (small or large)

The following will describe the type of meeting and how it could best be conducted:

- Routine meeting – open approach
- Emergency meeting – guided discussion approach
- Information-sharing meeting – round-robin approach
- Problem-solving meeting – interview approach
- Decision-making meeting – stand-up approach
- Planning-meeting – walk and talk approach

- Evaluation meeting – telephone approach
- Combination meeting – internet, with or without video approach
- Brainstorming meeting – teleconference approach
- Motivational meeting – lecture or instruction approach
- Spontaneous meeting – discovery, discussion, or decision approach

Middle managers spend approximately eighteen hours per week in meetings, but only half of these meetings are considered to be productive. Meeting problems include:

- late start or end
- the leader is not prepared
- no agenda or they do not follow agenda
- poor environment or distractions
- no visuals or poor visual aids or equipment
- participants arrive late or leave early
- unclear objectives or expectations
- participants do not know how to participate

Planning can greatly enhance the effectiveness of a meeting. Plan the following:

- roles – what individuals need to do to have a successful meeting
- types – what kind of meeting is needed
- methods – how the meeting should be conducted

The meeting facilitator or leader should lead and be sensitive to difficult situations like latecomers, dominating personalities, being too friendly of a neighbor; and the silent personality. Techniques of effective meeting facilitation include:

- Clearly defining the meeting objective
- Explaining the facilitators role
- Encourage participation
- Give information to clarify details

It is wise to have a recorder keep a record of agenda items, delegated tasks, and decisions.

You also need a time keeper to foster awareness of time and progress. The meeting planner should develop a detailed agenda for the meeting facilitator with:

- Date
- Title
- Purpose of the meeting
- Desired results
- Location and contact information
- Scheduled time
- Meeting cost
- Meeting type, Method, and Role Assignments
- Participant list

The following quotes may help crystalize and clarify how meetings can be more helpful:

"A meeting is a gathering of two or more people for the purpose of reaching a common objective."
- Richard Winwood, *Creating Quality Meetings*

"A meeting is nothing less than the medium through which managerial work is performed. That means we should not be fighting their very existence, but rather using the time spent in them as efficiently as possible."
- Andrew S. Grove, *High Output Management*

"A management team will never function effectively in its meetings unless all members learn to carry out certain important functions and assume certain responsibilities."
- Dr. Thomas Gordon, *Leader Effectiveness Training*

"Everyone should know what to expect before coming to a meeting. You must be explicit about what's going to happen, how the meeting is going to be run, who is to play what roles . . ."
- Doyle and Straus, *How to Make Meetings Work*

"Meetings don't just 'happen'! Meetings are an ongoing part of organizational progress. Consequently, what happens prior to and, particularly, after a meeting is more important than what happens during the meeting."
- Arlen B. Crouch

Chapter 9

Demand Accountability

*"It is wrong and immoral to seek to escape
the consequences of one's acts."*
- Mahatma Gandhi

Responsibility and Accountability

Accept responsibility for your life, your duty, the problems you create, and the challenges that come with these. Diagnosis is one thing. Finding and implementing a cure is another. People must stop doing certain things and start doing other things. Beliefs dictate actions that produce results.

Give your wholehearted commitment and draw forth the same from others. Results are the product of the way people think and act which is their culture. Individuals and groups will perform at its highest potential only if they personally accept the responsibility for achieving the desired results. Their action is motivated by changing their beliefs as a result of experience.

To achieve the desired results, an organization's culture must be aligned with the results. Alignment means agreeing to move in the same direction once a decision has been made, whether or not we agree with that decision.

Great management is the art and science of getting things done through others. Great leadership is managing the way people think and act. This is not an event or a program, but an ongoing process. Be great by taking responsibility and holding yourself and others accountable and to be disciplined. The word discipline comes from the same root as disciple. Kindness or giving attention, appreciation, and encouragement is what discipline means.

We are accountable to see, own, solve, and do.

We are accountable to *see* by:

1. obtaining the perspectives of others
2. being open and candid in our communications
3. asking for and offering feedback
4. hearing the hard things.

We are accountable to *own* by:

1. being personally invested
2. acknowledging our involvement
3. creating and maintaining a sense of alignment
4. owning both the personal and the team's objectives.

We are accountable to *solve* by:

1. constantly asking, "What else can I do?"
2. actively redefining boundaries
3. creatively dealing with obstacles
4. staying focused on results.

We are accountable to *do* by:

1. reporting proactively
2. relentlessly following up
3. doing the things we say we will do
4. measuring our progress toward achieving the intended result.

Commitment

We are all accountable to our creator. We are accountable to ourselves. We are accountable to the government in the country, state and community in which we live. In each case, we have a choice to be accountable and decide to commit ourselves to this end. In a large degree, our accountability is intimately related to our commitment. The greater the commitment is, the more effective and reliable the accountability will be. The greater the commitment is, the greater the results will be. When we are committed, greatness will flow to us and flow from us. The following quote says it all:

> " . . . *Until one is committed there is hesitancy, the chance to draw back, always ineffectiveness. Concerning all acts of initiative (and creation), there is one elementary truth, the ignorance of which kills countless ideas and splendid plans: that the moment one definitely commits oneself, then providence moves too. All sorts of things occur to help one that would never otherwise have occurred. A whole stream of events issues from the decision, raising in one's favor all manner of unforeseen incidents and meetings and material assistance, which no man could have dreamt would have come his way. I have learned a deep respect for one of Goethe's couplets: 'Whatever you can do, or dream you can, begin it. Boldness has genius, power and magic in it.'"*
>
> - W.H. Murray

There are three characteristics of a commitment. First, there is clarity of vision. Second, there is a dedication and a belief to act as if it is so even if it is not yet so. Third, there is a passion, which is excessive behavior. Personally, I don't want a job, I want a quest! I want something I can give myself to.

Help Others Be Committed

"The only people that can ruin a relationship or make that relationship work are the two people in it."
- Rob Liano

We need to help others to be committed. Some people are self-starters and can do it on their own. However, at times we all need help. When committing others, resolve to be bold in consistently committing people to do things that will help them to help themselves. However, we have the responsibility to cultivate discernment so you will not commit a person beyond their ability. Commitments progressively increase in difficulty according to the ability of the individual to accomplish the commitments. We should learn to commit people when the time is right.

There are many techniques or steps in becoming skilled in committing people. Assume people will commit. It is important that the person you are committing verbally commits to do what you are asking him to do. There is seldom a need to say, "I want to commit you to so and so." Just commit them! Express your confidence them and their ability to keep their commitments. Assure people that they are not alone and there is help available. Do not be afraid to promise people success as they follow through on a commitment.

If someone resists making a commitment or fails in keeping a commitment, find out why by asking questions, listening, and use your common sense and intuition. Sometimes the excuses expressed are not really the problems.

Always follow up on commitments made by others under your care or leadership. Refer specifically to the commitments and discuss how your children, team or employees have done. If others are not doing their part, first look to yourself and evaluate your own responsibility regarding the matter. But, don't make their problem your problem. If we are positive and do all in our power, then many people will be benefited by making and living up to their commitments.

Commitment is a basic ingredient of success. It first must begin with us. We must ask ourselves, "Am I committed? To what am I committed? To what degree am I committed?" Remember the old Vermont farmer who said, "You can no more teach what you ain't got, than go back to where you ain't been."

A Balanced Life

Enjoy your life. Enjoy your work. Sometimes, it's seems like we are running faster and faster on a treadmill and getting farther and farther behind. We must live and act and be from something deep in our heart. Our heart is more than a pump. It's our spiritual center. Heart is courage and compassion. Without it, life is empty and lonely, and we will always be busy, but never fulfilled.

Stop Worrying

Concentrate intently on your business and responsibilities during working hours, but never worry about these things during the evening. There is a world of difference between planning and worrying. Remember what the purpose of your work or business is. Do not forget yourself, your family, your country, or your religion. It is so easy to get caught up in the excitement and sport of business that often the business activity dominates what is most important in our lives.

Smell the Flowers

My wife frequently reminds me to "smell the roses along the way." Impoverished is the man or woman who loses themselves or their family to an all-consuming desire to succeed or achieve other professional ambitions.

At times, it's important to get away from it all. Value your time away and alone. Take plenty of time off. Take time alone for prayer and reflection. Get enough sleep. Take vacations. Real vacations are ones in which you truly do get away from your routine work. As important as it is for you to get away, it is just as important for your family, friends, and fellow workers to get away from you!

Times of Renewal

"Sounds become music in the spaces between notes, just as words are created by the spaces between letters. It is in the spaces between work that love, friendship, depth, and dimension are nurtured. Without time for recovery, our lives become a blur of doing unbalanced by much opportunity for being."
- Loehr & Schwartz, p. 34

All spiritual, mental, physical and emotional aspects of your life are interrelated. We live in exciting times and can do exciting things. There is a lot of stress, but stress is also good. There needs be stress and opposition in all things or we couldn't progress. However, chronic stress and distress is not good. The difference is how we view and deal with it. It's healthy to enjoy a challenge, but it's not healthy to let a challenge consume or overwhelm you.

We all need moments, days and times of renewal. An important part of renewal is one purpose for the Sabbath day. Spencer W. Kimball said, "Jesus . . . taught us how important it is to use our time wisely. This does not mean there can never be any leisure, for there must be time for contemplation and for renewal. . . ." We should all be anxiously engaged in a good cause and do our very best. We should also make time and take time to renew ourselves and recharge our batteries.

Balance and Recovery

It is this balance and recovery and these "spaces between work" that requires focus and attention. With all we have on our plate, sometimes life can become very stressful. Have you ever felt like Lucille Ball in the Chocolate Factory, just trying to keep up with the workload?

We should work hard and then relax. Deal with stress and then recover. We need to do much the same as athletes do when exercising or performing. The example athletes use to make this point is the difference between the sprinters and the long distant runners. The sprinters are muscular and robust. The long distant runners are thin and gaunt and weak in appearance. The difference is that the sprinters go as hard as they can and then rest. The long distance runners are paced. They just keep going and going – like the Duracell rabbit. This may not be the best example, but it helps us to visualize the point.

For us to be robust and healthy, we need to work hard and fast and then take time to recover. Prolonged stress can have negative effects on our attitudes and health. However, even in long periods of stress we can do a lot, depending on how we react.

Occasionally, we just feel stuck. Perhaps we don't get closure on certain things and don't have an opportunity to celebrate the completed task. Perhaps we can celebrate more often. Perhaps we could step back and examine the situation. We could pray alone or together over the problem. Perhaps we can congratulate each other or pat each other on the back more than we do. We can do this in hundreds of different ways in private or in public. I believe we can be happier and reduce stress by celebrating small achievements.

Life Planning

Planning is taking future events and bringing them into the present. Regardless of whether we feel like we are racing through life or just plodding along, we can regularly step back to evaluate our long term goals and objectives. We can ask ourselves, "Why am I doing this? What is my purpose and what matters most? How can I stay focused on the things that matter most?"

People can have their own life plans in place so their daily activities will compliment what they want to be. When our behavior is congruent with our ideals and beliefs, we can realize true happiness and success. We can be great and foster greatness in others. For the purpose of discussion, I will refer to this life plan as a "Personal Productivity Plan."

Personal Productivity Plan Components

In order to develop a personal productivity plan, you should consider several components. Such a plan includes ideals, values, principles, and processes. As described earlier, the basic components of a personal productivity plan are as follows:

- Life's Mission Statement (what you want to be)
- Governing Values (the things that matter most)
- Long Term Goals (desired results measured in lifetime, 3-5 or 10 years)
- Intermediate Goals (desired results over a short term, 1 year or less)
- Daily Tasks (desired results to be accomplished today)
- Tools (to describe and measure the concepts and progress)

Affirmations, Goal Setting, and Prioritization

"To everything there is a season, and a time to every purpose under the heaven."
- Ecclesiastes 3:1

Affirmations are the way we state reality to ourselves and others. They are positive statements about what we are or want to be even though we are still working on being or becoming. Our affirmations can be positive and help develop our self-esteem. There are so many voices that seek our attention and time. For example affirmations may read as follows:

- "I avoid extremism—and remember commitments to family and church."
- "I spend more time with family."
- "Motherhood is my most important responsibility."
- "I am professional and successful in my job."
- "I am a good neighbor and friend."
- "I am involved politically and serve my community."

131

Balance and Harmony

The proportion of time a person spends in various activities differs significantly, depending on the particular phase of life. Each season of our life has a special purpose, and fulfillment comes through experiencing each season's purpose at the proper time.

Sometimes we get depressed and ask, "When will it ever end?" There will always be demands, but our depression will decrease when we accept the fact that coping with demands is a natural part of life. It doesn't help to just escape them. It helps to face reality and live happily one day at a time.

Let's look at an analogy: When a bicyclist pumps his legs, the bicycle moves and the rider remains balanced. But if he doesn't pump and the bicycle slows down and then completely stops moving, the rider loses his balance and falls over. The same is true when we are depressed or perplexed. By remaining inactive, waiting for the many demands to come to an end, we begin feeling sorry for ourselves, and our perspective becomes distorted. Movement and activity, on the other hand, help us maintain balance and keep our lives productive and in proper perspective.

To find harmony in our lives, we must learn to take control of the various demands on our time. Consider the analogy of a choir director. By taking control over the specialized interests of each vocalist, the director turns confusion into a balanced, melodic hymn. The same is true with the varying "voiced demands" in our lives. Rather than allowing these voices—all of them good—to determine their favorite hymn and volume, we must expect each demanding voice to wait its turn. We have the ability to be agents to act rather than just be acted upon. It is our responsibility to control the balance as we exercise our agency to act. Learning to do this is the object of our existence.

Nature can life your spirit and touch your heart. You find your soul by contemplating nature and looking deep within. There you discover your spiritual center. The journey of the soul is a quest through uncharted territory. Begin by asking where you are right now and where you should be going.

Environment

The relationship we humans have with life is expressed by E.O. Wilson, one of the world's great biologists: "If all humanity disappeared, the rest of life (except for pets and house plants) would benefit enormously. Forests would restore themselves, endangered species would slowly recover, and, in general, all life might breathe a sigh of relief that we're gone. However, were any other major species to disappear, for example, ants, the results would be that major extinctions of other species and probably partial collapse of some ecosystems." The whole earth would suffer if it lost any other species except humans.

One of the biggest flaws in our approach to life is the Western belief that competition creates strong and healthy systems. Television programs show animals locking horns in battle or ripping apart their prey. It is true that in any living system there are predators and prey, death and destruction. But competition among individuals and species is not the dominant way life works. It is always cooperation that increases over time in a living system. Life becomes stronger and more capable through systems of collaboration and partnering, not through competition.

We aren't often told what happens to ruthless predators, but it's a story we need to know. When a new predator appears in an ecosystem, it acts greedily, consuming far more than its share of available resources. Its greed disturbs the system's balance. Many local species die because their habitat is destroyed. But after a time, the system self-corrects. Either the rapacious species dies off because it has destroyed its food supply, or it calms down, learns the rules of the neighborhood, and consumes fewer resources. Other local species are able once again to thrive. A healthy ecosystem is always composed of many diverse species living together as a network of cooperation. Each member of the network eats from a specific part of the food web, and leaves the rest for others.

The Web of Life

Today, too many of us have forgotten that we live in a web of life. However, the knowledge of our proper role has been held and taught by many indigenous peoples. Their traditional teachings can help us remember that, in this web, we are welcomed as family members, not as greedy consumers.

We may also have forgotten that every species is essential to the entire web. We believe we can destroy those species that threaten or annoy us, and no harm will be done anywhere else in the web. We still act surprised when efforts to eliminate one pest end up turning fertile fields into clay or desert, destroying birds, frogs, and thousands of species in the soil, air, and water. We not only kill the pest, we also destroy all those species that are essential to healthy fields.

Life will continue to teach us that we can't make up our own rules. There's only one way to run this planet, and life is pushing back forcefully right now, insisting that we learn this. We are experiencing dramatic and frightening climate changes all around the globe, destructive floods, more deserts and barren soil, new diseases and pandemics. We can't continue to pretend or insist that our modern ways of relating to earth's web of life are working to maximum efficiency.

We need to learn how to be good neighbors. I believe the easiest way to become partners with life is to get outside, to be in nature and let her teach us. About half of us no longer have this option. Half of the world's population lives in large cities, breathing polluted air, unable to see the stars, never knowing peace or quiet. I grieve for those of us who cannot know the feel of wild places, the sound of a small stream or the shade of a grove of trees.

For those of us who still have nature available to us, it is even more important that we get outside. We need to experience the power and beauty of life on behalf of all humans who no longer can do this for themselves.

On behalf of those who cannot, we need to feel the power of a storm against our faces, the fury of the wind, the cycles of destruction and creation that are always occurring. We need to experience sunlight shining off swamp grasses, to sit with the sunset, to rest under a tree, to go out in the dark and look up to the stars. If we can do these things, we will fall in love with life again. We will become serious about sustaining life rather than destroying it. And our commitment will help all those others who can't ever know what they're missing.

Charles Darwin, who interpreted life's evolution as a battlefield of competition, death, and struggle for survival, had paradoxical sensations when he was outdoors in "the smiling fields." He could feel the peace and harmony of the fields, even though his work described warfare. In his journal, he wrote: "It is difficult to believe in the dreadful but quiet war of organic beings, going on in the quiet woods and smiling fields."

If we spent more time outside, letting life teach us, we would change our relationship to the earth. We would remember what it feels like to be part of life. We would understand the sentiments of Fiona Mitchell, a twenty-two-year-old college student in England who surprised herself by becoming an ecological activist:

"I'd love to be able to just get on with my life and enjoy it and do the things I want to do . . . And it's really annoying that you can't get on with your life because the planet is being destroyed. But I, personally, can't just ignore it, because it's part of me. It is part of all of us, you know. I think a lot of people don't see the connections between things, the connections that run through everything. We have to take care of everything, because it's all part of the same thing."

Address Poor Performance

Let's turn our attention back to responsibility. We must handle corruption immediately. We can profit by Jesus' example of dealing with the moneychangers in the temple in Jerusalem. When he observed the activities of these extortionists and usurers, he didn't call for a committee meeting. He didn't put the problem on the agenda for the next board meeting. He immediately and forcefully drove them out. This is a powerful lesson for all of us. When there is clear, irrefutable evidence of corruption anywhere, move immediately to handle it.

Habit

"Sow a thought, reap an act; sow an act, reap a habit; sow a habit and reap a character."
- James Allen

Our thoughts grow into action. Our actions repeated often enough become habits. Habits define what we do and often who we become as they mold our character. Bad habits need to be eliminated. Good habits need to be developed. Habits can be our best friend or our worst enemy. Great people work hard at developing good habits.

"I am your constant companion. I am your greatest helper or heaviest burden. I will push you onward or drag you down to failure. I am completely at your command. Half the things you do you might just as well be turned over to me, and I will do them quickly and correctly. I am easily managed--you must merely be firm with me. Show me exactly how you want something done and after a few lessons I will do it automatically. I am the servant of all great men; and alas, of all failures, as well. Those who are great, I have made great. Those who are failures, I have made failures. I am not machine, though I work with all the precision of a machine plus the intelligence of a man. You may run me for a profit or run me for ruin, it makes no difference to me. Take me, train me, be firm with me, and I will place the world at your feet. Be easy with me and I will destroy you. Who am I? I am habit!"

- Anonymous

Work Ethic

"Work is a blessing from God. It is a fundamental principle of salvation, both spiritual and temporal. . . . We are co-creators with God. He gave us the capacity to do the work he left undone, to harness the energy, mine the ore, transform the treasures of the earth for our good. But most important, the Lord knew that from the crucible of work emerges the hard core of character."

- J. Richard Clarke

High quality work is a matter of integrity, and every piece of work is a portrait of the one who produces it. Give an honest effort to your job as though you owned the enterprise. Each person is in business for himself, no matter who pays the wage. Always invest in your personal development and teach others what you know to help them progress, too.

Any system that does not require initiative, self-reliance, and the necessity of work for what we receive will not preserve the integrity of the individual. Work hard, work smart, and do your best. Work at completing the task at hand, but also work at doing the job well. There are weighty decisions and there are split-second decisions. If we develop the process and habits of good decision-making, our course will be sure and true.

If you are rich, share with the poor. If you are poor, you should also work. Don't wait to be told what to do. Every person should be anxiously engaged in a good cause, and do many things of their own free will. You have the power to do good things. Don't idle away your time. Don't neglect your natural talents. Eat by the sweat of your brow.

"We have a moral obligation to exercise our personal capabilities of mind, muscle, and spirit in a way that will return to the Lord, our families, and our society the fruits of our best efforts. To do less is to live our lives unfulfilled. It is to deny ourselves and those dependent upon us opportunity and advantage. We work to earn a living, it is true; but as we toil, let us also remember that we are building a life. Our work determines what that life will be. . . . Work is honorable. It is a good therapy for most problems. Work is the antidote for worry. It is the equalizer for deficiency of native endowment. Work makes it possible for the average to approach genius. What we may lack in aptitude, we can make up for in performance."
    - J. Richard Clarke

"If you are poor, work. If you are happy, work. Idleness gives room for doubts and fears. If disappointments come, keep right on working. If sorrow overwhelms you, work . . . When faith falters and reason fails, just work. When dreams are shattered and hope seems dead, work. Work as if your life were in peril. It really is. No matter what ails you, work. Work faithfully. . . . Work is the greatest remedy available for both mental and physical afflictions."

  - Korsaren

"The happiest man is he who has toiled hard and successfully in his life work. The work may be done in a thousand different ways; with the brain or the hands, in the study, the field, or in the workshop; if it is honest work, honestly done and well worth doing; that is all we have a right to ask."

  - Theodore Roosevelt

"It is never any benefit to give out . . . to man or woman, money, food, clothing, or anything else, if they are able-bodied, and can work and earn what they need. To give to the idler is as wicked as anything else. Never give anything to the idler. Set the poor to work."

  - Brigham Young

"Let us realize that the privilege of work is a gift, that the power to work is a blessing, that the love of work is success."

  - David O. McKay

Chapter 10

Leadership Builders

"Control is not leadership;
management is not leadership;
leadership is leadership."
- Anonymous

Be a Leader, Coach, and Mentor

People tend to focus on weaknesses. The first principle of leadership is authenticity and being an example. A great leader is also a teacher, and one of the greatest tools in teaching is example. Be flexible and value the culture you are in. Develop the skills to visualize change, create change and make change a priority. Be sensitive to timing and hold others to their commitments. It's wise to identify others who can be champions. Change is an evolution and not a revolution and good performance should be rewarded. Isolate those who think they don't have to change.

To lead you must be willing to serve. Don't use a power system, but do use a great deal of influence or authority. Your influence will live long after you are gone. Authority is always built on service and sacrifice.

Gandhi also personally served and sacrificed a great deal for the cause. He was imprisoned and beaten for his acts for civil disobedience. He went on long fasts to draw further attention to India's plight. Finally, in 1948, not only did the British Empire give India its independence, but they welcomed Gandhi in downtown London with a hero's parade. He did it through influence.

Dr. Martin Luther King recognized he didn't have power. Others, like Malcolm X and the Black Panthers, tried to fight with power, but power begets more power, and when they tried to use power they found greater opposition to their cause. The genius of Dr. King was that he claimed he could achieve civil rights for blacks without resorting to violence. Many laughed at him.

Authority built on service and sacrifice is simply the law of the harvest. You reap what you sow. If you serve me, I'll serve you. If you go to the wall for me, I'll go to the wall for you. Think about it. When someone does us a good turn, don't we feel naturally indebted? Leadership that is going to go the distance over the long haul must be built on authority. Authority is always built on serving and sacrifice, which is motivated by love.

When we meet the needs of others we will, by definition, be called upon to serve and even sacrifice. Who then is the greatest leader? They are the ones who have served the most.

Giving Others a Leg Up

We can all learn from each other. We should seek out good advice from others, and we can all help others in their needs. It is always helpful to have an independent perspective to examine, diagnose, prescribe and, if needed, perform surgery. It is healthy to listen to seasoned experts who can evaluate, analyze, and recommend. In turn, you can strengthen someone's weaknesses and help their strengths become overwhelming advantages.

Leaders and Followers

Everyone is a leader, and everyone is a follower. Leadership equals service and sacrifice. Leadership training should help to develop attitudes and skills in serving others. Few are born leaders. They are learned skills that are acquired by following examples of others. The best leaders are the best followers. The greatest is the least . . . and the least shall be the greatest. Lead by following. Be #1 by being last. Oliver Goldsmith said, "People seldom improve when they have no model but themselves to copy.

Correction should be an action of choice. It will most often be necessary when pride and arrogance get in the way of worthy goals and objectives. Rebukes are reserved for those you care about and respect the most. The receiver of the rebuke must know that there is a reservoir of goodwill and respect and that it is larger and more permanent than the rebuke.

The origins of the following quotes about leadership are not known, but their message rings true:

"The problem with being a leader is that you can't be sure whether people are following you or chasing you."

"No matter how high a man rises, he must have someone to look up to."

"You cannot lead anyone anyplace you are not going yourself."

"If not by me, then by whom. If not now, when?"

"A lot of people are like wheelbarrows — not good unless pushed. Some are like canoes — they need to be paddled. Some are like kites--if you don't keep a string on them, they will fly away. And many are like the North Star — there when you need them, dependable, ever loyal, in short, a never-failing guide."

Great Leaders

"It's not the cry, but the flight of the wild duck that leads the flock to follow."
- Chinese Proverb

Some prominent leaders people mention include George Washington, Thomas Jefferson, Abraham Lincoln, Winston Churchill, Mahatma Gandhi, John F. Kennedy, and Martin Luther King. These men were leaders, and they exhibited great qualities of wisdom and courage while they were performing on the stage of history. However, there have been great leaders in every nation and from every culture. In almost all cases they accepted the responsibility of their role, but were able to control the authority they had as a leader.

Generally speaking, it is the nature and disposition of almost all people, when they get a little authority, to forget their responsibility and begin to dominate others, thereby abusing their power. Great leaders learn to overcome this weakness and replace this tendency with qualities like persuasion, love, kindness, respect for truth, and purity of thought and action. They refrain from being hypocritical and guilty of living a double standard. Part of their strength lies in appropriately correcting others and then showing afterwards that they care. In this way, the person who is corrected appreciates her leader and his support, and devotion for that leader increases.

As I learn more, I am coming to realize that some of the greatest leaders in the world, especially in my life, were people very close to me. These leaders include my father, mother, former teachers and mentors. Their goal was to inspire me, lift and build me up so I could then do the same for others. As I learn more about great leaders and qualities and skills of leadership, I recognize a dimension that most of the world overlooks. The word that best describes this quality or attitude is "stewardship". Great leaders see themselves as stewards who have a responsibility to serve others, protect them, and teach them.

Everyone has greatness within whether they are going to school, raising a family, or working in business, science, education, politics, religion, or social science. They are great because they are committed. Commitment is what transforms a promise into reality.

Lincoln was a regular person who was committed.

"He failed in business in 1831. He ran as a state Legislator and lost in 1832. He tried business again in 1833 and failed again. He had a nervous breakdown in 1836 and ran for state elector in 1840 after he regained his health. He was defeated for Congress in 1843, defeated again for Congress in 1848, defeated when he ran for the Senate in 1855, and defeated for vice presidency of the United States in 1856. He ran for the Senate again in 1858 and lost. This man never quit. He kept on trying until the last. In 1860, this man, Abraham Lincoln, was elected President of the United States."
 - Anonymous

Interpersonal Skills

"People skills" include communication, motivation/ inspiration, positive relationship building, collaborating, and being open and receptive to new ideas. A person with great people skills responds positively to feedback, effectively resolves conflict, influences their leaders, peers and subordinates, builds the self-esteem of others, and teaches others in a helpful manner. There are power combinations in these various skills where one enhances or amplifies the other. Great leaders do many things well.

Beliefs

Nothing changes behavior more quickly than the adoption of a new belief. Not all beliefs are equal. Some beliefs are easy to change, some not so easy and some based on meaningful experience are almost unchangeable. People change as they form new beliefs. Create a belief statement that will be reflected in what you say to others. It should be a product of a desired state as if you already believed it, in the form of an affirmation. When we believe like this we can find lost items, solve difficult problems, soften hardened hearts and repair damage done.

Power-oriented people are generally threatened by authority-oriented people. Things can get uncomfortable. Nevertheless, there are few places where we cannot treat people with love and respect, in spite of how we are being treated.

Be Inspirational

Be a cheerleader as well as a coach. Share your vision with knowledge and authority. Tell your story with enthusiasm. Practice good public relations. A good advance man can prepare the way for the one for whom he is working. It is a very important role. Timing is very important. The advance person must understand timing, deadlines and relationship to news and be able to seize the moment.

Don't sugarcoat the truth. Don't promise an easy path. Most people can handle most situations when they have been honestly prepared to face them. Present things honestly and realistically. Don't oversell. Let others know exactly what lies ahead for them. If it is long hours, lots of travel, belt-tightening, let them know. Let them step up to the challenge of tough times. Lead into the future with eyes wide open, ready to tackle what lies ahead.

Teaching

In his book, *The Future Executive*, Harland Cleveland points out that "Every executive is a teacher." It has been said, "Give a man a fish and you feed a man. Teach a man how to fish and you feed a nation." By teaching we see that the recipient can help himself and others. By only giving we will see that the recipient will always want and need more.

In a similar manner, by giving only authority without training and understanding of responsibility, there is a great danger for the recipient to only want more authority and power. History shows so many who have not been able to achieve the right balance.

Teaching is in reality the basic process of selling. Selling is the process of influence and teaching. During a sales call, the President of the Connecticut State University told me that he was no more than a salesman. He said that any CEO is a salesman who was trying to sell his ideas and influence his group to the right end.

My father was an educator and planted in my mind and heart a tremendous respect for teachers and the impact on their students. It has been my privilege to be instructed by some of the world's greatest teachers, mentors, and leaders. Also, I have observed others who fell short.

> *"Be leaders of growth, not stewards of stagnation."*
> - Gordon B. Hinckley

Value of an Idea

Great people produce and champion great ideas. What is the value of a simple idea? Over the many centuries past, can we begin to measure the power or the expanse of ideas that have moved individuals and nations toward their destinies? It has been said that an idea may be more powerful than the strongest army or economic and political force. Such powerful ideas create this strength and guide these forces. The world is hungry for such ideas.

Be great! Beget and ponder great ideas. Be a supporter and champion of great ideas.

Remain Calm in the Storm

You can remain calm and still be fully engaged and actively involved. Plan for tough times, and have crisis plans ready to implement when needed. Use prayer to prepare and to help you through times of crisis.

It is important to treat others exactly the way you want them to treat you. The great paradox is "to lead others you must serve". All of us are much wiser than any one of us alone, and together we can make progress. One rule: If you feel moved to speak then speak, but if you are not moved then refrain to allow others to speak. Listening is one of the most important skills to develop.

Whenever two or more people are gathered together for a purpose there is an opportunity for greatness. You *manage* things, but you *lead* people. Leadership is the skill of influencing people to work enthusiastically toward goals identified as being for the common good.

A skill is simply a learned or acquired ability. Leadership is a skill set that can be learned and developed by anyone with the appropriate desire coupled with the appropriate actions.

There is a difference between power and authority. Power is the ability to force or coerce people to do your will, even if they would choose not to. Authority is the skill of getting people to willingly do your will because of your personal influence. Power is defined as ability while authority is defined as a skill. Power can be bought and sold and taken away. Authority cannot be bought or sold, given or taken away. Authority is about who you are as a person, your character, and the influence you've built with people. Power erodes relationships. Authority builds relationships.

Involve Others in the Decision-Making Process

Involving others in planning allows opportunities for growth. If you can't make up your mind decisively, then it will be more difficult to be great. Opportunities come and go. Being able to know when to make quick decisions is an important skill. Turn decisions into action and results. Dialogue is not decision making. Decide how to decide. Separate dialogue from decision-making. Make it clear how decisions will be made, who will be involved and why. Be clear about the line of authority.

There are four kinds of decision methods:

1. <u>Command</u> is where decisions are made with no involvement whatsoever of those under them. It's not their job to decide what to do, but to decide how to make it work.

2. <u>Consult</u> is a process whereby decision makers invite others to influence them before they make their choice. They gather ideas, evaluate options, make a choice, and then inform the broader population. Don't pretend to consult if you are not going to really listen to what others feel.

3. <u>Vote</u>. Voting offers the most efficiency is the highest value when you don't want to waste time. Votes should never replace patient analysis and healthy dialogue.

4. <u>Consensus</u> is often a horrible waste of time, but it can also be the most valuable method. This is where you need to jointly make a decision that each person agrees to support.

Don't take turns getting your way. Make the decision based on which proposal best meets the needs of the situation or group. Don't engage in post-decision lobbying. This is being both inefficient and disloyal. Once you've decided on something as a group, support the idea even if it fails.

Associates expect to be involved. They want to be empowered, to think, and take responsibility. When you give assignments, follow up! Assign a name to every responsibility. If you assign two or three people, then appoint one of them as the responsible party. Clarify up front the exact details of what you want and what you don't want (contrasting). Document your work. Hold people accountable. This will create a culture of integrity.

149

Counseling with Councils

Individuals, families and smaller groups can use support groups to discuss ideas, consider options and to help make decisions. Large organizations use focus groups or councils. The council can be a very useful device. The essence of the process is to get the right people engaged in vigorous dialogue and debate, infused with the brutal facts and guided by critical questions. The Council consists of a group of people who are key members of the decision making body and they participate in debate guided by critical questions about vital issues and decisions.

Our engines must be tuned properly. People, who become like an overworked cylinder in a car engine, will soon burn out. No one should be left to do it alone. A good system of committees and councils will support delegation and seek solutions in the best way. Counsel openly and listen to each other with profound respect for the abilities and experience of others. Discuss openly and respect differences of opinion. But, once a decision is made, always be united and determined. By doing this, we begin to understand how ordinary men and women can become extraordinary leaders. The best leaders are not those who work themselves to death trying to do everything single-handedly. The best leaders are those who plan and counsel with their councils.

"In cutting a diamond, we first look long and carefully at all sides and angles, and, at a given moment, the decision to cut must be made—with good or bad results. The whole difficulty of the operation—and consequently, the chances of success—lies in this work of analysis and preparation. If several people pool their knowledge and experience at the time of decision-making, the chances of meeting with failure are lessened and the chances of success are multiplied." Harold Geneen, former CEO of ITT.

Leadership Succession

A great leader's duty is to prepare for and train his successor. Remember in most organizations that everyone will either be promoted, demoted, fired, move to another company, change careers entirely, retire, or die. Prepare for these eventualities in a timely, systematic, measured, unselfconscious way. Some executives perpetuate the myth that they are immortal and that their presence is permanent. You and your organization deserve it.

To inspire others you must have faith in the people, and then you provide them with the resources they need. A leader is someone who identifies and meets the legitimate needs of people, removes all the barriers, so they can achieve the best results. Decide who will receive leadership development. It is important to develop leaders by defining the desired balanced improvements, results and strategies. This is not an end, but a means to an end.

Teach, Teach, Teach

"Be a teacher. Be a hero." Jesus Christ was the greatest of all teachers. He was often called *rabbi,* which means *teacher,* and he taught constantly. Great leaders don't hide in executive suites, plotting strategy. They find ways to teach, to inculcate those around them with their business ideas and ideals. Be like Jesus. Be a teacher. Be a success.

Field test your team. Give them specific tasks and then let them go do them. If you have taught them well and have given them clear and specific instructions, these will be times of learning and growing as well as times of advancement for your enterprise. Send them two by two to help each other. Don't be vague or general in making assignments.

Be an Example

Example is a true principle of leadership One of my favorite poets, Edgar A. Guest, expressed it so vividly in the verses of his poem, "The Sermons We See".

> *The eye's a better pupil and more willing than the ear.*
> *Fine counsel is confusing, but example's always clear.*
>
> *The best of all the preachers are the men who live their creeds.*
> *For to see good put into action is what everybody needs.*
>
> *I can soon learn how to do it if you'll let me see it done.*
> *I can watch your hands in action, but your tongue, too fast may run.*
>
> *The lecture you deliver may be very wise and true,*
> *But I'd rather learn my lessons by observing what you do.*
>
> *For I might understand you and the high advice you gave*
> *But there's no misunderstanding in how you act and how you live.*

Ralph Waldo Emerson said, "What you are, thunders so loud, I cannot hear what you say." You cannot lead anyone else further than you have gone yourself. When you help someone up a hill, you find yourself closer to the top. Benjamin Franklin said, "There is a difference between imitating a good man and counterfeiting him."

Someone wrote: "Example sheds a genial ray which men are apt to borrow."

So first improve yourself today and then your friends tomorrow. Be ready to do your part. Act decisively, be bold and do your part well.

Horatius at the Bridge

Great people seemingly cause the tide to rise, and that tide lifts all boats. This principle is dramatically described in the epic poem, "Horatius at the Bridge" by Thomas Babington Macaulay. There are moments in time when true greatness and courage shine forth for the whole world to see. Such was the case with Horatius with his two brave companions, Spurius Lartius and Herminius. Attitude, timing, and action make all the difference. The story is as follows:

Lars Persona of Clusium and his massive army of 80 thousand foot soldiers and 10 thousand horsemen were burning village after village on their way to conquer Rome. For two days and two nights they marched onward, clouds blackening the sky by day and flames lighting up the sky by night. Then a scout rode swiftly back into the city to report to the Fathers of the City that he was nearing the city just on the other side of the swollen and raging Tiber River.

The Consul could see the swarthy storm of dust rise fast along the horizon. The trumpet's war cry was heard repeatedly, and then the long lines of spears and helmets could be seen. Disheartened, the Consul admitted that they would be overrun before they could destroy the bridge across the river to stop their foe on the opposite bank. Then brave Horatius, captain of the gate, spoke up and said, "To every man upon the earth, death cometh soon or late. And how can man die better than facing fearful odds, for the ashes of our fathers and the temples of his gods? Hew down the bridge, Sir Consul, with all the speed ye may; I, with two more to help me, Will hold the foe in play. In yon strait path a thousand may well be stopped by three. Now who will stand on either hand, and keep the bridge with me?"

Without hesitation, Spurius Lartius and Herminius spoke up and stepped up to support Horatius in this overwhelming and certainly deadly challenge. The three soldiers raced to their position, tightening their armor while the Fathers, mixed with commoners, "seized hatchet, bar and crow to loosen the sturdy planks above and the strong props below." Meanwhile the enemy's ranks, like a sea of gold, surged and rolled forward toward the bridge's head. "Four hundred trumpets sounded a peal of warlike glee." All eyes were on the bridge's gate "where stood the dauntless three." They waited calm and quiet and watched the vanguard stop and listened to the loud laughter that rose throughout the ranks. Then three chiefs rushed forward, dismounted "before the mighty mass." They drew their swords, "lifted high their shields, and flew to win the narrow pass."

First, came Aunus of Tifernum. who was hurled into the river by Lartius and then "Herminius stuck at Seius, and clove him to the teeth; At Picus brave Horatius darted one fiery thrust, and the proud Umbrian's gilded arms clashed in the bloody dust. But now no sound of laughter was heard amongst the foes. A wild and wrathful clamor from all the vanguard rose. Six spears' length from the entrance halted the mighty mass, and for a space no man came forth to win the narrow pass.

But hark! The cry is Astur: and low! The ranks divide; and the great lord of Luna comes with his stately stride. Upon his ample shoulders clangs loud the fourfold shield, and in his hands he shakes the brand which none but him can wield." With his broadsword in both hands, Astur rushed at Horatius and "smote with all his might."

With his sword and shield, Horatius was able to turn the blow, but the blade came down and "gashed his thigh." A cry went up at the sight of blood. He reeled and momentarily rested on Herminius and then "like a wild cat made mad with wounds, sprang right at Astur's face. Through teeth and skull and helmet so fierce a thrust he sped, the good sword stood a handbreadth out behind the Tuscan's head."

With a heel on his throat, Horatius pulled out his sword. The Roman crowds on the distant banks cried for the three to return before the bridge fell. "Spurius Lartius and Herminius darted back; and, as they passed, beneath their feet they felt the timers crack." Safely across they turned to see brave Horatius standing alone at the gate. They started back across, "but, with crash like thunder, fell every loosened beam, and, like a dam, the mighty wreck lay right athwart the stream." A long shout of triumph and relief rose from all the walls of Rome, but no one could help Horatius, who stood alone against the massive foe.

"Down with him!" cried false Sextus, with a smile upon his pale face; "Now yield thee," cried Lars Persona, "Now yield thee to our grace!" Then Horatius slowly turned around without responding and looked to the white porch of his home, "O Tiber! Father Tiber! To whom the Romans pray. A Roman's life, a Roman's arms, take thou in charge this day!"

"So he spake, and, speaking, sheathed the good sword by his side, and with his harness on his back, plunged headlong in the tide. No sound of joy or sorrow was heard from either bank, but friends and foes in dumb surprise" watched as he sank and rose. With blood flowing and "heavy with armor, and spent with changing blows," he struggled on and finally felt his feet on solid ground. In victory, he was carried out and above the joyous crowd with shouts and clapping and weeping loud.

Focus on Strengths

John Flaherty sums up Peter Drucker's thinking, "Human performance capability depends on strengths and not on weaknesses. Of course, weaknesses have to be acknowledged and neutralized. Employees should be paid only in consideration of their strengths, not their weaknesses. To make strengths productive is the unique purpose of the organization.

When people know better, they will do better. Feedback and reward is critical in progress. Results are sometimes immediate and sometimes delayed. People need to know that what they are doing is appreciated and helpful to others. There is value in people being able to deliver difficult messages to each other in a constructive way. The healthiest feedback in organizations comes when people can freely exchange views with each other.

Some executives say it is lonely at the top. Who are they trying to please, the customer or their boss? Maybe the pyramid is upside down. Maybe the customer needs to be at the top. The role of leaders is not to rule and lord over others, rather to serve. Perhaps we lead best by serving.

Unfortunately, too many managers spend their careers getting in the way instead of getting obstacles out of their way.

Many are like the "Seagull Manger" who periodically flies into the area, makes a lot of noise, dumps on people, maybe eats their lunch, and flies away." Great managers must add value to the product of service and not just add to overhead.

Distilling Focus

"Here is the very heart and soul of the matter. If you look to lead, invest at least 40 percent of your time managing yourself - your ethics, character, principles, purpose, motivation, and conduct. Invest at least 30 percent managing those with authority over you, and 15 percent managing your peers. Use the remainder to induce those you "work for" to understand and practice the theory. I use the terms "work for" advisedly, for if you don't understand that you should be working for your mislabeled "subordinates," you haven't understood anything. Lead yourself, lead your superiors, lead your peers, and free your people to do the same. All else is trivia."

   - Anonymous

Great leaders process all the intelligence they have into a few alternative focus points. This is a powerful and important process. They must weigh between familiarity and structure, short-term and long-term, creativity and discipline, trust and change, bureaucracy and efficiency, people and productivity, management and leadership, and between revenue and cost. All the complexities and ambiguities need to be made clear for everyone.

Case Study: U.S. Marine Corps

"Leadership is a potent combination of strategy and character. But if you must be without one, be without strategy."

   - General Norman Schwarzkopf

157

Marines excel in their ability to develop leadership, and no organization on earth has more experience in developing leadership than the military. An energized workforce is "any group of employees whose emotional commitment enables them to make or deliver products or services that constitute a sustainable competitive advantage for their employer." If leadership is ultimately measured by results, then an important intervening variable is the energized or mobilized workforce.

Tom Clancy wrote *Marine* and concludes that the Marines have come to utilize some extremely powerful leadership development practices. Marines have developed practical methods through which to make these things happen.

The U.S. Marine Corps has 226 years of experience in developing leaders. There are two leadership groups. Most officer candidates are recruited from colleges as the brightest and most qualified people they can obtain. Nine out of ten applicants are rejected, and the Marines will not accept high school dropouts or someone with a GED certificate. The recruiters contact over 250 young people to find one qualified candidate.

The Marines make no pretense of getting the best and the brightest young people coming out of our finest high schools and colleges as recruits. All the usual predictors of success are not generally present in this group of recruits. Yet many of them are transformed into effective leaders after a two- to three-year period of time, and go on to display remarkable leadership skills as their careers continue. The percentage of success and the short time involved far eclipse that of any private-sector organization.

Development begins with understanding the tasks required. Leadership is a team effort rather than a solo performance. The

Marines pair a highly seasoned noncommissioned officer with a newly appointed lieutenant and allow the two of them to work together for several months. This eliminates many mistakes. The new officer has a sounding board of a seasoned leader with whom to think about strategies or tactics. The commissioned officers learn to rely heavily on their staff of noncommissioned officers.

Everyone is on the team. Leaders will make the final decision, but they not only allow disagreement, they almost demand it. Everyone is expected to express concern about questionable decisions and orders, and one of the biggest mistakes an officer can make is to ignore or squelch such questioning. Involving others is not a sign of weakness.

Today, the most sophisticated leaders recognize that they are not expected to have all of the answers or to define the strategy of the organization by themselves.

Leaders must be able to cope with rapidly changing leadership patterns. Clarity creates trust. Leadership requires the use of peer discipline and pressure. Discipline ensures a deep commitment to the organization, to the unit, and to comrades. Leadership involves planning and performing under intense time pressure. Speed is of the essence. It's better to have a 70 percent solution immediately than a 100 percent solution implemented late. Leadership demands reducing complexity to manageable simplicity.

The Marines have the "Rule of Three" where they narrow many alternatives down to three choices. They analyze these and select one. Marines are taught to take time to define an order's "essence." They are taught to pause to determine their strengths and weaknesses and state clearly the assumptions and define actions they must not take and to share the information they need to execute the mission.

Marines understand that there are many effective leadership patterns. They try to see the potential in the person and bring it out. They observe the natural strength and then try to magnify the quality. Their emphasis is on helping potential officers find their own force and magnify their natural tendencies.

Organizational Culture

Shaping and reflecting organizational culture is vital. People are the firm's most important asset, so they need to know, own, and reflect the culture. This begins with individual confidence and self-esteem. There is no gulf between leaders and followers. Everyone can be great. Everyone should be trained to lead. Diversity should be encouraged, not discouraged. Personal worth and continuous improvement must be the heart of the culture.

The culture should help each individual to reach their highest potential and perform at their best level. "To be or not to be, that is the question, " wrote Shakespeare. To become or not to become, that's the real question! Life is a progressive process of finding out who we really are and succeeding at whatever we can conceive and becoming whatever we want to be.

Montessori Principles

The Montessori education principles and approach is a model for personal and group development. The aim of Montessori education is to foster competent, responsible, adaptive citizens who are lifelong learners and problem solvers. Learning occurs in an inquiring, cooperative, nurturing atmosphere. Students increase their own knowledge through self- and teacher-initiated experiences. Students learn by manipulating materials and interacting with other students. The individual is considered as a whole. The physical, emotional, social, aesthetic, spiritual, and cognitive needs and interests are inseparable and equally important. Respect and caring attitudes for oneself, others, the environment, and all life are necessary.

The Montessori teacher is educated in_human growth and development and observational skills to match students' developmental needs with materials and activities. This allows the teacher to guide students in creating their individual learning plan. There is an open-ended array of suggested learning materials and activities that empower teachers to design their own developmentally responsive, culturally relevant, learning environment. Teaching strategies support and facilitate the unique and total growth of each individual. Classroom leadership skills that foster a nurturing environment that is physically and psychologically supportive of learning.

A Montessori classroom must have some basic characteristics at all levels. Teachers educated in the Montessori philosophy and methodology appropriate to the age level they are teaching, who have the ability and dedication to put the key concepts into practice. A partnership with the family is considered an integral part of the individual's total development.

A multi-aged, multi-graded, heterogeneous group of students use a diverse set of Montessori materials, activities, and experiences, which are designed to foster physical, intellectual, creative, and social independence. The classroom uses a schedule that allows large blocks of uninterrupted time to problem solve, to see the interdisciplinary connections of knowledge, and to create new ideas. It also encourages social interaction for cooperative learning, peer teaching, and emotional development.

Greatness in the Home

"No other success can compensate for failure in the home."
- David O. McKay

It is in the home where we first learn how to work with others, accomplish tasks, delegate tasks, and how to ask for help. In the home, a loving, genuine concern for each individual should be the prevailing attitude. A good home environment can lead to the development of qualities that will help both parents and children be good leaders.

Each individual can develop feelings of self-worth in our family members by giving them opportunities to develop talents and perform tasks well and then praising and encouraging their efforts. Children develop a sense of confidence as they are assigned to help with tasks that they are able to accomplish.

It is in our homes where we first learn to talk with others and to accept suggestions, where we learn how to resolve conflicts and overcome difficulties. We can learn in our homes to follow good role models and to be good examples for others. As parents, we must set an example of serving with good attitudes. These good examples will encourage our children and others to learn how to become great.

It is important that children be supported and encouraged in their responsibilities. Neal A. Maxwell said, "Making a place in our home life to teach, informally, leadership skills, can make it possible for our children to make a place in their hearts and lives later for the duties and challenges of leadership." The home is the incubator of greatness.

Our home garden will produce what we really want it to produce only as we use the tools to bring forth the greatest harvest. The same principles that have provided such a bountiful harvest in home gardens will also taking root in church, business, and community service.

Stretch Yourself and Others

The problem isn't how much you know, it's what you do with what you know. Great performers are not always those with the highest IQs or most knowledge, but those who perform their work differently. They developed strong networks and work with others. They help colleagues solve problems and complete tasks. They give others credit for success and express a desire to hear others' ideas. They do not impose their ideas on others and are genuinely concerned about others' personal needs. They bring out the best in others and work quietly without fanfare, putting the objectives of the team before their own. They are able to express complex ideas in lay terms and not hide behind jargon. They are scientific, persistent, skillful, imaginative and intelligent.

People do not intentionally attempt to compromise their integrity and tarnish their character. Honesty is the striking feature of the relationship between self-development and integrity. People who value self-development have the ability to evaluate and acknowledge their strengths and weaknesses. They learn from both success and failure. They carefully observe and study how things happen. They are value and understand cause and effect relationships.

In order to set stretch goals, you must believe in the stretch capacity of people and be effective at risk taking. Challenging the status quo and taking risks can convince others that they can achieve an almost impossible goal. Sometimes attitudes precede actions, but frequently actions need to precede attitudes.

Experience

Create and reinforce the positive experiences, beliefs, action, and results of the past. The current culture will persist until enough new experiences cause it to shift. Consciously manage these experiences. Reflect on their impact and what led you to form or change beliefs.

People tell one another stories that perpetuate culture. People will begin to look for these experiences and notice them. When one learns something new, they want to share it.

There are four types of experiences: 1) meaningful ones that need no explanation; 2) those that need interpretation in order to form desired results; 3) insignificant ones that have no impact; 4) those that are always misinterpreted regardless of interpretation. Most experiences are type 2.

Mel Bacon said, "The best way to exercise power is to give it up." Give advice rather than give approval. Great leaders renounce their own authority rather than consume it. Saying it doesn't make it so. It is better to change beliefs and actions by creating new experiences. You will either manager your culture or your culture will manage you.

When you give power away you wind up with more. Believe in yourself and others and expect excellence and success, and that's what you'll get. Expect failure and you will find that, too. Look for the good in others and have faith in them. If you do this, I promise that you will find greatness and see miracles happen in their lives and in yours.

Decision Making

Decision making is a process of making choices and then choosing how to act on those choices. We make decisions every hour of every day of our lives. If we develop the skill of being decisive it will help us throughout our lives. When faced with decisions, we can ask: What are my choices, consequences, or rewards? Do I have too many choices? Does it really matter? If I do not make a decision, what are the consequences?

The following suggestions will help the reader in making individual and group decisions:

Individual Decisions:
1. Define the challenge and the alternatives.
2. Study it out in your mind.
3. Make a decision! (Accept responsibility for your choices.)
4. Seek wise counsel. (Experts, parents, friends, God etc.)
5. Put the decision on the shelf for a time.
6. Revisit it, and if you feel good, go with it. (Commit)
7. Act on your decision. (Plan, prioritize, set goals, and work.)

Group Decisions:
1. Identify a leader for the group.
2. Define the challenges and the alternatives.
3. Freely and openly discuss all aspects.
4. Try to get consensus of the group.
5. Look to the leader to define the final decision.
6. Support the decision as your own.
7. Act on the decision.

Fatherly Advice

Whenever I would ask my father to help me with a problem or decision, he would usually say, "When confronted with difficult decisions, try this on for size; 1) Ask yourself what God would have you do. If that doesn't do it for you; 2) Ask what your father or mother (or some other role model) would do if faced with the same set of circumstances or difficulties. And finally; 3) Ask what you would want your son or daughter to do twenty-five years from now when they are your age and are faced with the same set of circumstances or choices. By doing this you will usually come up with some pretty good answers to your questions."

Leadership Quotes

"Being in power is like being a lady. If you have to remind people that you are, you aren't."
- Margaret Thatcher

"People cannot be managed. Inventories can be managed. People must be led."
- Ross Perot

"Leader: conductor, manager, director, guide, something that ranks first; a person that leaders have commanding authority; principle performer; the office or position of a leader; capacity to lead."
- Webster's Dictionary

"When the righteous are in authority, the people rejoice: but when the wicked beareth rule, the people mourn."
- Proverbs 29:2

"But it shall not be so among you: but whosoever will be great among you, let him be your minister; and whosoever will be chief among you, let him be your servant:

- Matthew 20:26-27

Chapter 11

Communicate Effectively

"Take advantage of every opportunity to practice your communication skills so that when important occasions arise, you will have the gift, the style, the sharpness, the clarity, and the emotions to affect other people."

\- Jim Rohn

Learn and Teach

We need to look like, think like, act like, and especially teach like real student and teacher. We need to be the real thing. A real life requires real learning, which depends on real teaching. Everyone has the responsibility to learn and teach.

Communication

Since the dawn of history, society has undergone dramatic changes in verbal communication. Technology, travel, and culture have had a lot to do with it. Much has been good, but there is still a lot left to be desired. Communication is the process of sharing understanding in a meaningful exchange through speech and behavior, using all forms of media. You should choose your words and forms of communication carefully.

If we have found any truth in the world and applied it correctly to our lives, we are growing in wisdom and we will be able to communicate more effectively with others.

My favorite poet, Edgar A. Guest, eloquently expressed this thought in the poem titled *"Wisdom"*:

> *This is wisdom, maids and men,*
> *knowing what to say and when.*
> *Speech is common; thought is rare,*
> *wise men choose their words with care.*
> *Artists with the master touch,*
> *never use one phrase too much.*
> *Jesus, preaching on the Mount,*
> *made His every sentence count.*
> *Lincoln's Gettysburg address,*
> *needs not one word more nor less.*
> *This is wisdom, maids and men,*
> *knowing what to say and when.*

Great communication requires empathy and understanding. The author, philosopher, teacher, and business guru Steven Covey teaches us to "First seek to understand, and then to be understood." This requires us to "walk in another's sandals" in order to understand them better and then become fluent in their language, whether it be baby talk, teengo lingo, any adult language, or body language. Our ability to communicate reveals our strengths and weaknesses. We are challenged, "If you're going to talk the talk then you've gotta walk the walk!"

Lifeline

Relationships are one of our highest a priorities in life. The lifeline of communication pulses through these relationships and gives them vitality and meaning. However, we often unwittingly damage or even sabotage them by allowing our emotions to determine our message or behavior. This can result in the loss of self-esteem for all parties involved, as well as deteriorating feelings for the relationship. We often say things we later regret and get caught in a self-defeating spiral of failure. This may not be recognized until it's too late.

At times, we allow ourselves to enter into or be pulled into quarrelsome debates or arguments when we could have enjoyed a stimulating exchange of ideas through healthy dialogue. Failure in healthy communication results in poisonous misrepresentation with all parties viewing the situation through their own biased shades of sunglasses. When this happens, our ability to influence others is greatly diminished.

Abraham Lincoln understood this and expressed it like this: "When the conduct of men is designed to be influenced, persuasion—kind, unassuming persuasion—should ever be adopted. It is an old and a true maxim 'that a drop of honey catches more flies than a gallon of gall.' So it is with men. If you would win a man to your cause, first convince him that you are his friend. Therein is a drop of honey that catches his heart, which, when once gained, you will find but little trouble in convincing his judgment of the justice of you cause, if indeed that cause really be a just one.

"On the contrary, assume to dictate to his judgment, or to command his action, or to mark him as one to be shunned and despised, and he will retreat within himself, close all the avenues to his head and his heart; and though your cause be naked truth itself, transformed to the heaviest lance, harder than steel, and sharper than steel can be made, and though you throw it with more than Herculean force and precision, you shall be no more able to pierce him than to penetrate the hard shell of a tortoise with a rye straw. Such is man, and so must he be understood by those who would lead him, even to his own best interests."

Productive Communication

When the issues are important and we have strong feelings about something, it is even more important to have productive communication. These 'alive' conversations happen on a daily basis and have huge impact on our ability to progress individually or lead other people or groups in their progression and development. If we want to influence others and bring about change through our leadership, we must constantly improve our communication skills. This affects every aspect of our lives at home, work, school, church, in the community, etc.

John Powell said, "Communication works for those who work at it." If we learn to control our thinking, emotions, and behavior we can enjoy more peace of mind, better health, a stronger family, more lasting friendships, and a richer life. Good thinking is important, but doing is better. Great people teach others what they themselves are trying to do.

If we encourage others to enthusiastically participate, they will contribute and be accountable for what is shared and the way it is shared. For example, studies show that couples who are honest and respectful with their partners have a much higher quality of relationship and a greater chance of success and staying together.

Withdrawing, brooding, and other silent behaviors undermine the relationships and possibly result in violent behavior. We must learn to watch for and recognize the signs of unhealthy communication and act positively. This takes effort and appropriate practice. We should always be actively practicing developing our relationships.

Communicate the Big Picture

You must create a climate of truth in order to be heard and to confront brutal facts. Winston Churchill said, "We are resolved to destroy Hitler and every vestige of the Nazi regime. From this, nothing will turn us. Nothing! We will never parley. We will never negotiate with Hitler or any of his gang. We shall fight him by land. We shall fight him by sea. We shall fight him in the air until, with God's help, we have rid the earth of his shadow."

You must maintain unwavering faith that you can and will prevail in the end, regardless of the difficulties, and at the same time have the discipline to confront the most brutal facts of your current reality, whatever they might be. It is impossible to make good decisions without infusing the entire process with an honest confrontation of the brutal facts.

Creating a climate where the truth is heard involves basic practices of leading with questions, not answers. It involves repeatedly asking why, why, why? You must engage in dialogue and debate, not coercion. You will have to conduct autopsies, without blame, and then build red flag mechanisms that turn information into information that cannot be ignored. Hit the realities head-on and face the hard truths by saying, "We'll never give up. We will find a way to prevail." Develop a stronger will to live and avoid an attitude of victimization.

You must never confuse faith that you will prevail in the end, which you can never afford to lose, with the discipline to confront the facts of your current reality, whatever they might be. Strip away the noise and clutter and just focus on the few things that would have the greatest impact. One of the primary ways to de-motivate people is to ignore reality.

Poise

Stay in dialogue even when you are angry, scared, or hurt. People react differently to the same stimulus. You and only you create your emotions. You can act on them or be acted on by them. Just after we observe behavior and just before we feel emotion is when we add meaning and judgment. Based on these thoughts or stories in our mind, our body responds with an emotion. We see and hear and then tell a story. We then feel and then act. It is in telling the story or telling a different story that we control our emotions. Shakespeare said, "Nothing in this world is good or bad, but thinking makes it so." It is our interpretation of the facts that help explain what we see and hear.

This happens blindingly fast. If you want to improve results, change the stories you tell yourself, even while you're in the middle of the fray. Slow down and take charge of your path to action. Stop and notice your behavior. Take an honest look at what you are doing and what you feel. Analyze, think about it, question if you are right and change if you are not. Admit weakness and begin corrective action.

Separate fact from story by focusing on behavior. Either our stories are completely accurate or they're quite inaccurate and justify our current behavior. "It's not my fault!" In victim stories we exaggerate our own innocence and ignore the role we played in the problem. "It's all your fault!" In villain stories we overemphasize the other people's guilt. It's a double standard when we assume the worst.

"There's nothing else I can do." In these helpless stories we make ourselves out to be powerless to do anything. We tell ourselves that there are no healthy alternatives, which justifies the action we are about to take.

These stories excuse us from any responsibility. We do this after we failed to do something we knew we should have done. We must retrace our path and ask: "What would I do right now if I really wanted these results?" and "What would I do right now if I really don't want these results?"

Turn to One Another

We can change the world if we listen to one another. Human conversation is the most ancient and easiest way to cultivate the conditions of personal and global change. We move at a frantic speed. The world encourages us to love things rather than people, to choose fear instead of peace. Conversation takes time, and it's not easy.

Human beings have always sat in circles and councils to do their best thinking and to develop strong and trusting relationships. We have to slow down, think, learn, and get to know each other. We need to simplify our lives.

There is no power equal to a community discovering what it cares about. Real change begins with the simple act of people talking. It only takes two or three. We are hungry for a chance to talk, tell our story, and listen to others. This helps us not to feel isolated, strange, or invisible. We don't have to start with power, only passion. When we don't talk, we give up humanity and freedom.

Great people acknowledge one another as equals and stay curious about each other. They recognize that we need each other's help to become better listeners. We must slow down to have time to think and reflect. We expect it to be messy at times. We must be willing to be disturbed. We can't be satisfied with superficial conversations where we pretend to agree with one another.

Leaving Comfort Zones

We must be willing to move into the very uncomfortable place of uncertainty. We can't be creative if we refuse to be confused. It's scary to give up what we know. Great ideas and inventions miraculously appear in the space of not knowing. If we can move through the fear and enter the abyss, we are rewarded greatly. New voices revive our energy, and oftentimes help us discover solutions to problems that seem unsolvable.

"I need to learn to value your perspective, and I want you to value mine. I expect to be disturbed by what I hear from you. I know we don't have to agree with each other in order to think well together. There is no need for us to be joined at the head. We are joined by our human hearts."

A sense of purpose helps us deal with whatever life experiences await us. If we don't have meaning, life's difficulties can easily overwhelm and discourage us. This sense of purpose beyond ourselves is a universal human experience, no matter our life circumstances. We don't have to be comfortable, well-fed, or safe in order to feel purpose in our lives. We become more fully human with any gesture of generosity, any time we reach out to another. We need to keep our hearts open. Anger causes us to feel less human.

We are creating the future every day by what we choose. The future comes from where we are now. We can change direction by changing thinking and behavior. We must develop the will to act once we know what to do. The gap between knowing and doing is only bridged by the human heart.

Ask Key Questions - Why, What, How, Where and When?

When few are willing to tell top management bad news that is desperately needed, you need to appreciate and reward those who will tell the truth, no matter how distasteful that truth might be. If you are only getting good news, you might not be getting the whole picture.

Jack Kinder says, "When you ask the right questions – when you monitor and measure what matters – performance always improves. Listen when others blow up or clam up. You can't take responsibility for someone else's thoughts or feelings, but you can do whatever it takes to retrace their paths to action. Be sincere and listen. When we show empathy and genuine interest, people feel less compelled to use silence or violence.

Dean Rusk said, "One of the best ways to persuade others is with our ears, by listening to them." By acknowledging others' emotions, we are saying that it's okay with them feeling the way they are feeling. The key is to remain calm and collected.

Sometimes we have to prime the pump by pouring some water into it to get it running. With power listening, sometimes you have to offer your best guess at what another person is feeling or thinking. This is an act of good faith where you take risks, become vulnerable, and build safety in hopes that others will share their meaning.

Presenting Opinions

Agree when you agree, and disagree when you disagree. Don't turn disagreements into debates. If you disagree, simply suggest that you differ by saying, "I see things differently." Don't turn differences into debates that lead to unhealthy relationships and bad results. Present opinions in a way that makes it safe for others to disagree.

There is importance in contrary opinion. Do not surround yourself with "yes" people. If everyone agrees on everything, then all but one are not necessary. Let people vent and understand that they have been heard. Then acknowledge and assume accountability for the situation. Finally, present a credible plan. People believe that a guide cannot lead them out of a situation they cannot acknowledge.

Fear

Be aware and keep a constant vigil on safety when it is at risk. Nothing kills dialogue like fear. By watching for the moment a conversation starts turning unhealthy, you can respond quickly and work your way back to healthy dialogue. Some of the conditions may be physical (stomach, heart, energy), emotional (fear, hurt, anger) or behavioral signals (raising voice, pointing finger, becoming quiet).

If you don't feel safe you can't take feedback, and even well-intended comments are suspect. When your emotions start cranking up, key brain functions start shutting down. Fight your natural tendency to respond in kind. Do something to make things safe and self-monitor and change your own behavior.

Make it safe to talk about almost anything and don't sugarcoat or water down the content of your message. Step out of the content of the conversation, make it safe, and then step back in. The first condition of safety is mutual purpose. Commit to seek mutual purpose or agree to agree and stay in this discussion until there is a solution both parties are happy with.

For example, my wife and I always had an open door policy regarding tough questions, but at least once a year, we would have a family council and talk about marriage, intimacy sex. We taught our children "the facts of life" and explained that we would answer any question they had. We told them that what we talked about was sacred and shouldn't be discussed outside of this council unless it was with us. They were not to discuss these things with their friends or among themselves without us being there.

Parable of Feedback

And the HR Specialist spoke to them a parable. Behold this feedback, and all other feedback. When the feedback is invited and freely given in a safe environment, ye see and know of your own selves that change is nigh at hand. So likewise ye, when ye see these things come to pass, know ye that great progress, desired results, and significant positive change is nigh at hand. Verily I say unto you, this management team shall not be promoted, until all be fulfilled.

Seek and Use Feedback

There are various kinds of feedback. Open feedback is the most important. Occasional feedback doesn't work very well. Unfocused feedback is better than no feedback at all, but specific feedback is the best.

People filter feedback and label it as inaccurate, dismiss it, or defend against it. If you don't respond to feedback, you stop getting it. People who give or receive feedback in the context of "perspectives being shared, "rather than "truth being declared" tend to manifest greater openness.

The best response is, "Thanks for the feedback!" A better response if the idea is useful is, "Great idea! I'll do it." Criticism will cause others to avoid giving or getting feedback. Positive and constructive responses to feedback are valuable. Ask, "What feedback do you have for me?" or "What do you think?"

Political correctness stifles productive feedback. Feedback should come in many forms and styles and from many different sources. In our "politically correct' world, there is a huge growing silent majority including those in the workforce that just follow because they are afraid or just need a job. Political correctness is not leadership nor does it foster greatness. It is political bullying and it is destructive.

People want the truth, the whole truth, and nothing but the truth. There are terrible results from an unsafe environment. People do what they are rewarded to do and they do things to get pleasure and avoid pain. Some people will rationalize and tell a lie even when the truth will do. Most, however, really do want to do the right thing

Steven Covey said, "To be trustworthy means you are worth of my trust." You need to gain feedback from all perspectives. By receiving timely, accurate information you can make adjustments, seek support, and be faster and more accurate with your decisions. It's a must! Be truthful, honest, and trustworthy.

Appropriately Sharing Information

Social culture including corporate culture is built primarily on the stories of both people and groups. It mostly includes stories of their success. Even corporate culture tells stories of business success and failure. Successful leaders tell these "war stories" over and over as a way of teaching how things are done. Speak persuasively, not abrasively. The best speak their minds completely and do it in a way that makes it safe for others to hear what they have to say and respond to it as well. Don't jump to hasty conclusions of victim, villain, or helpless story. Facts are the least controversial and most persuasive.

You don't need to apologize for your views or water down your message. Ask for others to share their views. Invite opposing views. Respect them and mean it. Play the Devil's advocate. The more forceful we are, the less persuasive we are.

Some don't merely speak, but try to force their opinions on others. Quite naturally, others resist. In turn the speaker pushes even harder to fight for the truth. Tone down the approach. Passion can be our enemy and can kill the argument rather than support it. "I can't hear what you say because what you do is thundering so loudly in my ears." You can hold to your beliefs; just soften your approach.

No Backbiting or Gossiping

Don't backbite or gossip. Don't do it! It is destructive and will poison your own well and those others need to drink from it. It will also poison the wells of others. When you need to quench your thirst, yours too will be ever so bitter.

Chapter 12

Service Oriented

"One trouble today is that so many people try to learn the tricks of the trade instead of learning the trade."

- Anonymous

Make Team Contributions

You lead with soul by giving to others. In Western culture it is the individual leader who must solve the problems for the group. In Eastern culture (Japan) it is the group's job to solve the problem for the leader. In Japan some executives spend time every week cleaning out the toilets. It's part of their gift.

An organization is ours, not mine. Sacrifice is setting aside our own wants and needs and seeking the greatest good for others.

Serving the Homeless

Spontaneous service is contagious, and it changes the world. It begins by changing us! When I think about this, I think about Jennie Dudley feeding the homeless in Salt Lake City. The following newspaper article was printed in *The Deseret News*:

They come by the hundreds on Sunday morning, down on their luck and hungry -- many of them without homes, some without hope.

Jennie Dudley feeds them under the viaduct near Pioneer Park on Fourth South. Nearly a hundred Sundays have come and gone since she began, but her basic equipment is unchanged: camp stoves and faith that God, through caring individuals, will provide food.

She never knows in advance what they'll be eating, or who will help her cook and clean up. Until the food arrives, she can't begin to guess how many hungry people will gather. "When there's a lot of food, I know we can expect lots of people. Somehow, praise God, there is always enough."

She began in a small way, with a camp stove, a coffee pot, a little coffee, a ball of fry bread, an iron skillet, and a little honey and butter. Hers was a solo act—for a few minutes. But someone drove by, asked what she was doing, and returned with food. It has worked that way ever since. "I don't try to organize things in advance," she said. "It's always provided, and it's never all fruit or eggs or meat. It's always a complete meal." Some weeks, she and other volunteers serve 600 or 700 people.

Unity

There is strength in unity.

- When many hearts and minds commit to a common purpose, their vision becomes reality.
- Success will always rely on our ability to foster collaboration and build alliances with each other.
- Working together means winning together.
- With synergy we can accomplish more than we could ever accomplish alone.

- Take responsibility for teaching each other.
- A chain is only as strong as its weakest link.
- By strengthening others you strengthen the whole.

Teamwork and collaboration allow common people to achieve uncommon results. As leaders we need to speak with one voice. Our hearts need to be knit together in one. If we are not one, we are on our own. We need harmony to go in the same direction at the same time.

Why Service?

A wakeup call from the soul is asking what life is all about. For everything there is a time and season. Now is the time to help someone else on their journey. Help guide others to greatness. Provide excellent service to others. I received some great advice from Richard L. Daft, an MBA professor at Vanderbilt University. When I was in his office, I asked him to briefly define leadership so I could go back and share with my MBA students. Without hesitation he said, "Service."

Dr. Daft thinks and teaches that greatness and leadership is all about service. The surest way to success is to put others first and become a servant to them in meeting their needs. Instead of following a model that says, "Let's pay these guys as little as possible and charge our customers as much as possible for the products we make as cheaply as possible so we can make as much as possible," he promotes a model that says, "Let's reward our people for providing the best products and services at the best price to our customers." This is the formula for success. In Matthew 23:11 we read, "He who is greatest among you shall be your servant."

Parable of the Lost Customer

And he spoke this parable unto them, saying, "What sales manager, having an hundred customers, if he lose one of them, won't get out of the office and bust his backside until he wins them back? And after he negotiates, he buys the customer dinner, and they sign a new contract. And when he gets back to the office he calls his sales team together and says, let's celebrate; I just won back the lost account! The whole company rejoices over the one lost account along with the ninety and nine loyal customers.

Glow Over the Phone

Marlo Payne is with Fidelity Title in Houston. I don't know much about her. I don't know what race, religion, or political party she is, but in just a few short conversations, I grew to appreciate her very much. Each time I've spoken to her, she's been helpful and very pleasant. But, more important, I've felt better after talking to her. She has a good spirit and just seems to radiate.

When I spoke to her one day, I asked her what it was that made her glow over the telephone. She laughed and shared her appreciation and then, in a softer voice she said, "I have to admit that I owe everything to God." I told her I understood and that she was a great example of excellent customer service. She's a great example of "Christ centered service". It's not just exceeding customer's expectations, but its doing it with the Spirit of the God.

Stew Leonard's Superior Customer Service

A few years ago, my wife purchased a large bag of oranges from Stew Leonard's, a local food store located off Exit 7 on

Federal Road in Danbury, Connecticut. Going through the bag, we noticed that there were half a dozen oranges that were overripe and spoiling. We agreed that it would only be fair to return them for six good ones.

When she returned from her errands, she was impressed about what she had experienced at Stew Leonard's. I overheard her telling someone on the telephone what had happened. She again related the experience to our family that when she asked for the exchange of the oranges, the young female clerk at the customer service desk insisted on giving her a whole bag of fresh oranges. Not six, but a whole bag full.

Mary-Jo said, "That's so nice, but just a fair exchange is all I expected."

"No Ma'am, just go and get another bag."

She left to make the exchange and pick up some apples and other items on the way. She probably ended up buying a lot more than she had expected to.

When she was paying at the cash register for the things in her cart, a young man came up and gave her a large bag of grapefruits with a sticker marked "Paid" over the $3.99 price tag. He said, "I want you to take this also in exchange for the oranges."

Surprised, she said, "You don't have to do that."

The employee replied, "Yes, please take it for your trouble."

She always loves to shop at that store, but you can imagine how good she felt that day. She has told that story to many of her friends. I have also told that story a half a dozen times, and it was the very thing that inspired me to write this book.

As a matter of fact, I'm enjoying some of that delicious fruit as I write. You know, that was the best advertising money the store could have spent. That bag of oranges and the bag of grapefruit sure went a long way—a very long way.

You know, this is the store I like to shop in almost any time. This family store has a great reputation for superior products and uncommon customer service. It's noteworthy to mention that people come from quite a distance to buy great produce and to have a unique shopping experience. The store is a huge barn, shaped with a children's petting zoo of farm animals at one end of the parking lot. If they ever ran out of parking, most people would walk across the street if they had to. I would, too.

When you walk in the front door, you pass a Wishing Well that invites you to donate the change in your pocket to a worthy charity. Can you imagine? Before you get in the door, they ask you to give your money away for nothing in return. Ah, but then you begin to experience shopping at Stew Leonard's!

That's when you see it carved in a huge two-ton granite stone right in the middle of the entrance way. You can't miss it. These are the two rules that the store lives by.

Rule #1: The customer is always right.
Rule #2: If the customer is ever wrong, re-read rule #1,
- signed, Stew Leonard."

In another location, on a large hanging sign, is Stew Leonard's Mission Statement that is "We work to make happy shoppers!"

Wow! What about that? Do you think they succeed 100 percent of the time? Probably not, but they sure are close.

Now, there are a lot of interesting stories about this place, and this one that helped form some of Stew's philosophy is hearsay, but I'll share it anyway. It is said that in the early days of his career, when they only sold milk and a few other products, one of Mr. Leonard's customers came back to return a carton of milk she thought was going sour. He immediately insisted on making the exchange, but then he made the mistake of opening the carton to taste it while the customer watched. Not thinking it was going bad, and maybe hoping to reassure the lady's confidence in their "freshest milk" label, he said something like, "You are certainly welcome to take another carton, but it tastes fine to me." With that, his customer became offended, and said, "I will never shop in your store again," and walked out. He had just told the lady that she was wrong and he later noted that he watched a $50,000 customer walk out of the door, and vowed never to make the same mistake again. Thus, he came down from his mountain with the rules written in stone.

You might ask yourself, as I did, "How could she be a $50,000 customer?" Well, Mr. Leonard figures that the average family in this area spends about $400 per month, or almost $5,000 per year, on the items he wanted to carry in his store. In 10 years of business, it adds up to over $50,000 of business. Everyone who walks into the door is a least a potential $50,000 customer. If they are a satisfied customer, their worth goes up by the number of others they bring in.

Immediately upon entering the large open doorway of the store, you smell the sweet aroma of freshly baked goods that is piped in just for such enjoyment. You begin to salivate, and no matter when you've last eaten, you're hungry all over again. The ice cream bar is on the one side and the popcorn treats and an assortment of flavored coffee beans on the other.

My favorites are all the free samples. As you go past the baked goods there are assorted samples of the most delicious muffins and cookies or little cups filled with samples of cherry or apple pies and plastic forks to eat it with. There may be samples of shrimp dip and shrimp at the seafood bar or ham, chicken or roast beef at the meat counter. Just enough to feel satisfied and leave you with the feeling that you want to come again.

It is fun to take visitors from out of town to Stew Leonard's just so they can share the experience. Recently I took my brother through when he came to visit while on a business trip. I said, "If I were a homeless person, I would live next door to this place and come here every day. I'm surprised that lots of other stores haven't duplicated what they are doing here.

The Leonard family started as a small dairy store with a limited number of items. They have grown much larger, but they keep that personal touch that keeps people coming back. Kids love to go there with their parents. It's like a small entertainment center. There are talking and singing chickens, cows and milk cartons that are started by pushing buttons that are easy to reach by the kids and a person dressed up like a cow just wandering around entertaining the kids both young and old. There's a whole generation growing up that will be shopping at Stew Leonard's for the rest of their lives.

Two years ago, my friend David Logie from Hartford stopped in at Stew Leonard's with his family on their way back from a weekend vacation in New York City. They had gone to see a couple of plays, the museums, and some of the tourist sites. He wanted to exchange some free ice-cream tickets someone had given him quite a while before. His whole family loved it. When they were again traveling east on I84 toward home, he asked the kids what they enjoyed most about the weekend. Almost in unison they enthusiastically responded, "Stew Leonard's!" He leaned over to me and said, "Can you imagine that? After all the planning and effort, to say nothing of the expensive hotel and other expenses that had totaled over several thousands of dollars, they liked Stew Leonard's the best, and I didn't have to spend a dime!"

Customer service is more than just providing superior products or services. It's all about how you make people feel and how they feel about you.

Ken Blanchard and Raving Fans

Raving Fans: A Revolutionary Approach to Customer Service, by Ken Blanchard and Sheldon Bowles describes four characteristics, or needs, for success in business:

1. Be customer driven, which means to focus on the customer
2. Be cost effective, which means that sales must exceed expenses
3. Be fast and flexible
4. Overcome inertia and manage change
5. Serve with all your might, mind and strength. Give it everything you've got!
6. Be continuously improving by always learning and getting better.

Blanchard suggests that a healthy company could also be compared to a three-legged stool, with integrity being the seat and the three legs being raving customers, happy employees, and financial strength.

The book also preaches that companies need to create "raving fans." Satisfied customers just aren't good enough. The secrets to creating raving fans are:

1. Decide what you want
2. Discover what the customer wants
3. Deliver more than you promise.

Under promise and over deliver. To create raving fans, don't drive promises down. Drive delivery up.

Blanchard continues by stressing how important it is that great people have their own vision. We must ask and then listen closely. We must discover who our customers are and what they really want. Customers don't just come to buy products; they come with problems that we need to find solutions for. We need to "create a vision of perfection" and to do that we must ". . . imagine perfection centered on the customer. . . ." Once we have a real vision, we need to bring down the picture from our mind and impose it over actions, individuals, and groups. "There's no such thing as too good, and there's no such thing as never. There's always a way to do it."

Blanchard goes on to define the magic ingredient as being "flexibility." The perfect vision isn't a frozen picture of the future. Customers' needs and wants change all the time. Your employees are the key to satisfying those needs and wants. "If you don't look after your people, they won't look after your customers. If you say thank you and reward them, they'll do it again and again. You must decide what you want and discover what the customer wants and then deliver that plus one."

"How do you go about finding out what my customer's vision is? . . . Ask them and then listen closely both to what they say and to what they don't say. But first you have to discover who your customers are.

"Customers care about everything . . . It's just that most of them haven't thought through their whole relationship with you, only some specific areas. Because customers are often so focused on a specific priority, it's easy to match up what they want with that area of your vision. But first you have to discover what they really want."

The test of reasonableness for a vision is "If it serves a customer need it's valid. There's no such thing as too good, as long as it's within what you choose to define as your window of customer service. And there's no such thing as never. There's always a way to do it."

Quality Quotes

"The most important moral of all is that excellence is where you find it. . . . We must learn to honor excellence, indeed to demand it in every socially accepted human activity, however low or exalted the activity. An excellent plumber is infinitely more admirable than an incompetent philosopher. The society which scorns excellence in plumbing because plumbing is a humble activity and tolerates shoddiness in philosophy because philosophy it is an exalted activity will have neither good plumbing nor good philosophy. Neither its pipes nor its theories will hold water."
- Anonymous

"True perfection of man lies not in what man has, but in what man is."
- Anonymous

"There is no glory in half-finished tasks."
- Anonymous

"We are haunted by an ideal life, and it is because we have within us the beginning and the possibility of it."
- Anonymous

"If a thing is done well, no one will ask how long it took to do it, but who did it."
- Anonymous

The Outback Experience

It was our first time eating at the restaurant known as Outback Steakhouse. We were quickly seated and noticed a nice dining atmosphere. Our waitress was exceptionally friendly and spent time going over the menu. Everything was brought quickly and we were excited not to have a long wait. The bloomin' onion was unique and delicious. We had black bread and a huge meal of salmon with French fries and filet mignon with baked potato and salad. The only complaint was that the non-alcoholic daiquiri could have been larger. My wife asked for her filet to be medium with red in middle, but it was over cooked. Immediately, the waiter left to get another one. Then a gentleman came to apologize and offered to pay for our dessert. Later, the cook came out and apologized and told us that we were right. The steak was too well done. A new steak and new fresh baked potato were quickly brought to my wife. Even though she had finished her potato, they insisted that she have another. The steak was brought out and they waited for her to cut it to see if it was cooked right.

My wife and I decided to order the Thunder Down Under chocolate dessert and enjoyed it too. When the bill came, they had given us the dessert for free. We told the waitress that when people were treated so nicely they would always come back. She sat down with us, and we told her the story of Stew Leonard's service. She told us about the owners and how good they were to the employees and how good they wanted to be to the customers. It is their philosophy, not just an isolated experience. Needless to say we left her a big tip!

On the way out, the hostess at the front desk opened the door for us and we commented on what a nice experience we had had and that we would be bringing our family back. She smiled and said, "That's what we are known for—Good Food and Good Service! Have a nice evening."

We talked about our experience on the way home and with our children at breakfast the next day. Customer service is not just getting what you expect and pay for, it's getting more than you expect and in a spirit that says "You are the most important person to us."

Chapter 13

Resolves Conflict

*"Whenever you're in conflict with someone,
there is one factor that can make the difference between
damaging your relationship and deepening it.
That factor is attitude."*

- William James

Constructively Resolve Conflict

In a personal, family, community, or business setting, you must constructively resolve conflict by:

1. directly focusing on the *issue*, not the *person*
2. helping participants stay neutral
3. not being devious
4. staying focused on the *issues* and not the *emotion*
5. keeping private things private

Anticipate Problems, Accept Responsibility, and Seek Solutions

Tragedy wounds our spirit. Wounds provide an eye to finding new possibilities. Humor is a wonderful heart song. You know enough about yourself and human nature to know that there will be conflicts to deal with and challenges to overcome.

Be prepared. Be prepared intellectually, emotionally and otherwise. When a conflict arises, take a deep breath, listen to understand all aspects before jumping to conclusions. Ask questions for clarification and be willing to receive the truth or what others perceive as the truth. Approach all parties with the proposition that there is a solution and everyone involved is exploring what the best solutions are. Many times, asking the right questions helps those in conflict to discover the solutions on their own.

Solve Problems

We all have problems, and that's good. A problem is the difference between what we have and what we want. Problems have lifecycles. Problems tend to go on until they get bigger and bigger and become a crisis or catastrophe. The best thing to do is to deal with them and learn from them. By learning from our problems, we turn them into opportunities.

Ed Kugler describes his "Corkscrew Approach" to solving problems:

1. Define the problem
2. Ask what happened
3. Ask why it happened
4. Ask what can be learned from what happened
5. Ask what we will do differently based on what we learned

It takes patience and commitment to reach the core of a problem. If we don't learn from our mistakes we are doomed to repeat them.

Yeah, But

Thomas Fuller said, "A man surprised is half beaten." Many problems and decisions catch us unprepared and off guard. A vast majority of these problems go away if they're privately, respectfully, and firmly discussed.

Deference, or what feels like kissing up, requires that you work on yourself as a leader first and discover your part of the problem. Go public and describe the problem and ask your team for advice. Don't try to command the problem away. Reward risk takers and encourage testing. Tentatively state what you see happing. If others play the game, call them on it. Don't use your mistrust as a club to punish people.

Keep Things in Perspective

See reality, keep things in perspective, handle one thing at a time and don't give up. Sometimes we forget our essence and have lost touch with our soul. Crisis brings us face to face with our soul. Some have sleeping sickness of the soul. When we live superficially, we pursue no goals deeper than material success, and never stop to listen to our inner voices. We block our spiritual development.

We need a new paradigm to move us beyond the traps of conventional thinking. Sometimes we have to get off the beaten path and explore. Lao-tzu said, "A good traveler has no fixed plans and is not intent upon arriving. A good artist lets his intuition lead him wherever it wants. A good scientist has freed himself of concepts and keeps his mind open to what is."

Many are looking for the image of an autonomous, lonely hero wandering on the fringes of society – a Lone Ranger,

Dirty Harry or Rambo. The spiritual journey that we must take, and inspire others to take, begins with ourselves, but not necessarily by ourselves. You can draw support from a circle of friends, a spouse, close colleagues, or a religious community.

We should develop spiritual disciplines or exercises such as prayer, meditation, studying scriptures, singing hymns, following prescribed rituals, journeying to sacred places, and contemplating nature. Be willing to compromise and agree on how to stay on track. Be willing to cut your losses. Don't let pride and stubbornness keep you where you don't belong, or doing something that will keep you from progressing, or in a relationship that is not going to work out.

Settle disputes quickly. Try to come to agreement before you get to court. Be a peacemaker and a catalyst for reconciliation. Turn to arbitration if necessary. Be tolerant of others and deal effectively with those whose background or viewpoints are different from your own.

Avoiding Debt

Greatness involves every aspect of our lives, including finances. It has nothing to do with how much money we have or how little we can give. It has everything to do with our attitude about and our behavior with money and what we do with it. We can look and live rich, but still be in debt or bondage. We can also look and live modestly and be free and wealthy.

In my opinion, Dave Ramsey is the Moses of leading people out of debt. I did a summary of his book, *The Total Money Makeover*, and sent it to all my children, family, and friends and invited them to read it and do everything he said. I've listed below some of the bullet points and guideposts he gives in leading us out of bondage and into the Promised Land of being debt-free and prospering. First, let me share some philosophical points about wealth:

Philosophy

- Personal finance is 80 percent behavior and only 20 percent knowledge.
- Financial principles are simple and time proven.
- Your biggest challenge is *you*.
- Do not try to keep up with the Jones; they're broke.
- It is painful to make changes.
- Debt is not a good financial tool to create prosperity, and it creates major risk.
- Living in debt is living in bondage.
- Money is an excellent slave and a horrible master. Money will work for you by earning interest unless you work for money by paying interest.
- The love of money, not money, is the root of all evil.
- By sacrificing now, you will receive blessings and prosper later on.
- Acknowledge your financial weaknesses.
- Study wealth and wealthy people and teach your children correct financial principles and practices.
- Plan and live for the future while you are living in the present.
- Envision financial freedom and build wealth to have fun, to invest, and to give.
- Always manage your own money.
- Maximize your investing.
- Avoid "Affluenza" by allowing wealth to become your God.

Dave Ramsey uses a number of scriptures from the Old and New Testaments to support his philosophy, practice, and recommendations. There are many others that could be included from other holy books, but let me share the following that he shared:

Bible Scriptures:

- Romans 12:2 *"And be not confirmed to this world: but be ye transformed by the renewing of your mind, that ye may prove what is that good, and acceptable, and perfect, will of God."*
- Proverbs 22:7 The rich rules over the poor, and the borrower is servant to the lender.
- Proverbs 17:18 It's stupid to guarantee someone else's loan.
- Proverbs 13:22 A good man leaves an inheritance to his children's children.
- Luke 14: 28 *"Which of you, intending to build a tower, does not sit down first and count the cost, whether he has enough to finish it . . ."*
- Proverbs 10:15 A rich man's wealth can become his walled city.
- Proverbs 6:1 and 5 *"If you have signed surety, my son, . . . deliver yourself like the bird from the hand of the fowler and the gazelle from the hand of the hunter."* (surety is debt)

Dave Ramsey gives 10 Commandments of "Do's" and also 10 Commandments of "Don'ts". Think about it. Learn it, live it, and do it. Teach and share it.

10 Commandments of Financial Prosperity (Do's)

1. Pay a 10 percent tithing to the Lord *(your church or charitable organization).*
2. Develop and work a budget every month *before it begins.*
3. Keep a $1,000 cash emergency fund and a 6-month emergency fund (in liquid assets) for unexpected expenses.
4. Get out of debt and stay out.
5. Save and invest 15 percent of your gross income.
6. Get an education:
   - Pay as you go,
   - Get scholarships,
   - Save in ESAs and 529s,
   - Look into the military. Ask your CPA about ESAs and 529s.
7. Pay off your home faster by using 15-year mortgages.
8. Pay for things in cash, including cars and if possible your home.
9. Buy appropriate insurance for auto, home, life, and health and long-term care.
10. Keep your retirement, will, and estate plan current.

10 Commandments of Financial Ruin (Don'ts)

1. Do not use credit cards, debt, college loans, debt consolidation, or a home equity loan (HEL) as financial tools.
2. Do not use cash advance, payday loans, rent-to-own, title pawning, and tote-the-note car loans.
3. Do not lease cars or have car payments.
4. Do not purchase whole life insurance, ARMs, or balloon mortgages.

5. Do not invest in gold, mobile homes, prepaid funeral expenses, or pre-paid college tuition.
6. Do not lend money to, or cosign loans for, friends or relatives.
7. Do not leave open debts in a divorce.
8. Do not gamble, play the lotto, or try shortcuts to prosperity or get-rich formulas.
9. Do not file bankruptcy or use debt management companies.
10. Do not raise your life style when you get a raise.

Stress Fitness

Life has purpose and meaning. It is our classroom to learn to reach our potential and become the great people we are destined to be. Why not make the best of it? As Ziggy says, "It beats all the alternatives."

Along with all the good things, life provides us with many challenges, obstacles, opposition, adversity, sickness, heartache, etc. etc. etc. Life is both joyous and difficult. Let's call our pressing forward through life, "stress." There is "good stress" and "bad stress." It's all for our benefit if we understand it, know how to evaluate it, and learn how to deal with it. So, let's begin with the decision to do just that.

Understanding Stress

Stress is a normal part of life and helps us develop, grow, and overcome. We experience stress at every age and stage of our life. It is a normal physical and emotional response to the changes and challenges in our life. Without it, we would never learn, overcome, achieve, help or heal. However, if we have too much for too long, it can cause us problems. Most stress is experienced in dealing with change and opposition. Opposition can come from any direction. Changes take place in every aspect of our lives. Thank goodness for both.

Stress comes in different forms throughout our lives. As children, we experienced a whole new world of sight, sound, speech, taste, touch and control. As teenagers, we became aware of learning, emotions, discipline, acceptance, self-esteem, dreams and disappointment. Then, as young adults, we transitioned to being responsible, becoming educated, getting new jobs, developing relationships, establishing goals and a family. Later, during those years of providing, we look after others, make our contributions to society, and share with others what we have experienced and learned. Finally, in old age, we struggle with the changes that come with retirement, aging, loss of health, and wondering why others don't seem to get it.

Levels of Stress

For simplicity, let's divide stress into four levels. This will help us recognize, evaluate and deal with stress in a more effective and productive way.

The levels will be called:

1. Good
2. Uncomfortable
3. Bad
4. Dangerous.

Periodically assessing your stresses and levels of stress will help you maintain balance and use stress to your advantage.

A *good* stress level would be when you are happy, confident, and ready to meet challenges. You recover quickly from setbacks, and your relationship with others and with God are healthy. Keep up the good work.

An *uncomfortable* stress level is when you feel tense, worried, or anxious, and you have trouble getting along with others and feeling God's love. Don't be hard on yourself. Relax and read some uplifting books or listen to inspiring music.

A *bad* level is evident when you are upset, emotional exhausted, easily angered and discouraged. Pray, search for solutions, and get help if this continues for more than three days.

The *dangerous* level requires immediate attention by seeking professional help. Whenever possible and at any level, you should take a break from the stress causers and make sure you are properly nourishing your body, mind, and spirit.

Kinds of Stress

General stress just comes with moving through life one day at a time. We will also experience *physical stress* depending on how much work or movement we do. It is also affected by our diet, our ability to rest sufficiently, and the safety and health of the environment we are in.

Our *emotional stress* level is manifested in our thinking and emotions. We experience emotional distress depending on our self-esteem, relationships and level of required activities.

Social stress is definitely related to our interaction with new people and our relationship with those we know.

On top of this, *intellectual stress* will be realized as we struggle to learn, teach, plan, manage expectations, adapt to change, and understand life itself.

Finally, *spiritual stress* can be the most challenging because it comes with trying to understand the universe, our life, who we are, where we came from before we were born, and where we go after this life. Is there a God and what is our relationship to all these other people in my house and on this earth?

There are valuable resources, principles, and practices to help us take advantage of the good stress and to reduce or manage the bad stress. The most valuable are relaxation, prayer, scripture study, and the influence of the Holy Spirit. But there are more that are also very important and helpful.

The best medicine for bad stress is work, uplifting activity, and helping others.

Response to Stress

Attitude is the most important element in how you respond to stress. Your perception of stress will determine how you process it and react to it. The results of your reactions will yield either strengthening or debilitating results. Think positive thoughts and change negative thoughts into positive ones.

Be aware that everyone in this world is dealing with stress. Be a good listener, smile, say kind things to others, and help them along their way. You can make the world a better place by making people happy.

Prayer and journal keeping will give you strength and help you learn from stressful situations. If you acknowledge God in all things you will feel His spirit influencing you in many ways. Serve others. The best antidote to relieve your pain is to help someone else with theirs.

Music has magic in it. Sing and listen to good music. Get plenty of exercise and rest. Eat well and don't take anything into your body or mind that is unhealthy. Manage your expectations, focus on what needs to be done right now. Don't try to control others or situations. Take regular breaks. Don't get down on yourself. Be grateful, have faith, and take one step at a time.

Being guided or guiding others to greatness requires that you become expert in managing stress. Start now to understand it and respond appropriately.

Chapter 14

Creatively Proactive and Initiative Driven

*"Sometimes creativity is pure genius,
and other times it is just good old common sense."*
- R. J. Wrigley

Be Creative

Our conscious and creative mind gives us wonderful riches. It is not the material things in life that bring joy, but the simple, valuable things that are free.

Be creative, and blaze new trails. Great people are open to the universe and do not let their imagination get stifled. R. J. Wrigley was on a plane once and the man seated next to him asked Wrigley why he continued to advertise so widely when his company was already the most successful maker and distributor of chewing gum in the world. "For the same reason that the pilot of this airplane keeps the engines running after we are already in the air," replied Wrigley.

Challenge Conventional Practices

Challenge conventional practices and search for new and more effective solutions. Take the initiative and get things done. Appreciate and adapt to changing needs.

Discover, plan for, and champion change in your personal life and in the organizations you are associated with. Translate your vision into meaningful goals and daily tasks. Always take the long view, and work to connect the outside world with your goals and with other people. Understand that strategic change will take you in new directions and that tactical changes or what specific thing you will be doing differently will help you personally and your organization perform better.

Change

See change and adversity as an opportunity and not a problem. Greatness is all about change. So if people are not producing change, then they are probably not doing things right. If one waits, nothing will happen. The strongest pressures impact people and change their strengths, pushing performance up or down.

Beliefs are the patterns, models, or maps we use to navigate our way through life. Great people continually challenge their beliefs, the world around them, their organizations, and other people. Sometimes our beliefs are not accurate. We see the world as *we* are. Others see us as *they* are. Change takes us out of our comfort zone and forces us to do things differently.

Continuous improvement is crucial for people as well as organizations because change is constant. It is impossible to improve unless we change. George Bernard Shaw said, "The reasonable man adapts himself to the world; the unreasonable one persists in trying to adapt the world to himself; therefore, all progress depends on the unreasonable man."

Parable of Opportunity

Now learn a parable of opportunity. When the recruit is yet new in the company and puts forth his best efforts, ye will know that a promotion is nigh at hand. So likewise, when ye see these things ye will know that it is near, even at the doors. Verily I say unto you, this annual performance review shall not pass, till all these things be fulfilled. Ineffective managers and employees shall be terminated, but that day and hour knoweth no man, no, not even his immediate supervisor, by the CEO only.

But as in the days of the reorganization, so shall also the organizational change be. For in the days that were before the reorganization they were wining and dining and playing up to their immediate supervisors, until the day that the pink slips were given out. And they knew not until the axe fell and they were unemployed. So shall the future changes be.

Then shall two be in the same office. One shall be promoted and the other let go. Two shall be doing their month-end reports. One shall get a raise and the other become an outsource consultant. Watch therefore, for ye know not the hour this will happen, but know this that if the employee had known in what day the virus would attack his computer, he would have watched and unplugged his machine. Therefore be ye also ready, for in such an hour as ye think not that opportunity cometh.

Who then is a faithful and wise employee, whom the boss has made manager over his company and given him compensation accordingly? Blessed is the employee who, when his boss visits, shall find him so doing. Verily I say unto you, that he shall make him manager over all his company. But if that lazy servant shall say in his heart, my boss isn't really interested in what I'm doing and never comes, and the servant begins to mistreat his workmates and to wine and dine his supervisor, the boss shall come in a day when he is not prepared and in an hour when he is not aware, and shall fire him on the spot. He will be unemployed and will blame it on his boss.

Commitment

> *"There is no chance, no destiny, no fate that can circumvent or hinder or control the firm resolve of a determined soul."*
> - Ella Wheeler Wilcox

"Until one is committed there is hesitancy, the chance to draw back, always ineffectiveness. Concerning all acts of initiative (and creation), there is one elementary truth, the ignorance of which kills countless ideas and splendid plans: that the moment one definitely commits oneself, then providence moves too. All sorts of things occur to help one that would never otherwise have occurred. A whole stream of events issues from the decision, raising in one's favor all manner of unforeseen incidents and meetings and material assistance, which no man could have dreamt would have come his way. I have learned a deep respect for one of Goethe's couplets: 'Whatever you can do, or dream you can, begin it. Boldness has genius, power and magic in it.'" W. H. Murray

Success in achieving a goal or greatness is preceded by a commitment to that end. A commitment is a pledge, or an agreement, to do something. Love is a very important ingredient in committing people to accept and live a principle, achieve a goal, or progress toward greatness. [I would clarify this—love of the idea? Seems far-stretched]

Faith is another prime factor in determining how people will respond to our request to participate, unite with us, sacrifice, and work toward a common goal. We can exercise and develop faith by learning to create a mental picture of people accepting and following through on such commitments. By repeatedly rehearsing in our mind what we want to accomplish we will recognize our level of commitment and dedication and gain the power and ability to commit others.

Resolve to be bold in consistently committing people to do things that will result in their progress and benefit. Commitments progressively increase in difficulty according to the ability of the individual to accomplish the commitment.

There are many techniques or steps in becoming skilled in committing people. First, assume people will commit. It is important that the person you are committing verbally commits to do what you are asking him to do. There is seldom a need to say, "I want to commit you . . ." just commit them!

If someone resists making a commitment or fails in keeping a commitment, find out why by asking questions, listening, and then perceiving through empathy. Always follow up on commitments in subsequent contacts. Refer specifically to commitments and discuss how they have done.

Be like a smart bomb with laser thinking, discipline, and flexibility. Commitment is a basic ingredient of success. It first must begin with us. We must ask ourselves, "are we committed?" Are you committed? To what are you committed? To what degree are you committed?

Summary

Every person has greatness within and can demonstrate it because:

Chapter 1: Essence of Greatness

1. They define the essence of greatness.
2. They possess divine attributes and qualities.
3. They acknowledge universal truths and principles.
4. Their own philosophy and behavior is in alignment with universal truths and principles.
5. They accept every person as being unique and special.
6. They have a passion for life, liberty, and pursuit of happiness.
7. They respect experience and yearn for adventure.

Chapter 2 Values Driven, Values Based & Goal Oriented

1. They are clearly focused on the organization's mission and vital purposes.
2. They are passionate about what they do.
3. They are goal oriented and self-motivated.
4. They have good planning habits and frequently review business plans.
5. They effectively manage their time and resources.
6. They are reasonable and use good judgment and control their emotions.
7. They seek to be re-energized.
8. They understand that happy people are more productive and creative.

211

Chapter 3 Founded on Integrity

1. They are honest and true at all times and in all things.
2. Their word is their bond and they consider their reputation sacred.
3. They are responsible and dependable.
4. They build positive energy and enthusiasm within their organization.
5. They accurately represent others interests when they are not present.
6. They treat all people with fairness and respect regardless of their position.

Chapter 4: Guiding Greatness

1. They are a guide.
2. They discover and demonstrate various dimension of greatness.
3. They bring out the greatness in others and orchestrate the talents of others.
4. They are striving to be great leaders.
5. They strive to stay focused on the most important things.
6. They always strive to improve.

Chapter 5: Relationship Governed

1. They network, develop alliances, and trust others.
2. They access and build on strengths in themselves and others.
3. They find the right person for the job and the right job for the person.
4. They love celebrating and rewarding others.
5. They are skilled negotiators seeking fair results for all parties.

6. They are financially compatible in earning, saving, spending, borrowing and investing.
7. They understand that partnership incompatibility can breed contempt, anger, frustration and separation.
8. They are quick to forgive and forget.
9. They are a compliment to their team members.
10. They know their people's background, strengths, weakness and financial status.
11. They know what they are willing to risk in their relationships.
12. They effectively accomplish objectives with people in other parts of their organization.

Chapter 6: Truth Seekers

1. They are teachable, willing to listen and seek advice before making decisions.
2. They are open-minded and seek new ideas through other's perspectives.
3. They seek divine inspiration and encourage others to do likewise.
4. They align their decisions and behavior with truth and proven principles.
5. They choose to think positively and be optimistic.

Chapter 7: Excellence and Quality

1. They set measurable standards of excellence for themselves and others.
2. They focus on both performance and results.
3. They get people to stretch and reach goals beyond their expectations.
4. They are obsessed with excellence and focus more on quality than quantity.

5. They define success as achieving what they want while enjoying what they have.
6. They are continuously improving in every area.
7. They learn from mistakes and make proper adjustments.
8. They are creative, innovative and act outside the box.
9. They are always trying to improve faster than the market demands.
10. They monitor, measure and analyze performance and progress.
11. They focus on the 20 percent effort that gives 80 percent of the results.

Chapter 8: Think Strategically

1. They approach things strategically.
2. They always anticipate their next move and adapt to change.
3. They know what they want and how to get it.
4. They have alternative plans and a well-planned exit strategy.
5. They do the right things rather than just do things right.
6. They adopt appropriate systems approaches, but they don't forget people or flexibility.
7. They are calculated risk takers and wise risk managers.
8. They understand the value of timing.

Chapter 9: Demands Accountability

1. They are responsible and accountable to themselves and others.
2. They are balanced in their approach to life.
3. They address poor performance in a timely manner.

4. They hold themselves and others accountable for responsibilities and producing results.
5. They accept responsibility for problems.
6. They have a strong work ethic.

Chapter 10: Leadership Builders

1. They see themselves as a leader, coach, and mentor.
2. Their job is to have vision, ideas and give direction, motivation and inspiration to others.
3. They have courage to be decisive even when doing so carries personal risk.
4. They are decisive and involve others in decision-making process.
5. They include co-workers in presentations and meetings.
6. They focus on developing others to become leaders.
7. They understand how their decisions affect others.

Chapter 11: Communicate Effectively

1. They effectively bring up issues for consideration when receiving input from others.
2. They work at communicating the broad picture instead of just on a need to know basis.
3. They ask key questions about expectations concerning the whys, how, where and what.
4. They present opinions in a way that makes it safe for others to disagree.
5. They actively seek and make effective use of feedback from others.
6. They appropriately share information openly and honestly.
7. They refrain from backbiting and gossiping.

Chapter 12: Service Oriented

1. They make significant contributions toward achieving team goals.
2. They work for the benefit of the whole rather than just personal interests.
3. They help others understand how they contribute to the organization's mission.
4. They support and enable others to do their jobs.
5. They provide excellent service to internal and external customers.
6. They cheerfully do their share of new or disagreeable tasks.

Chapter 13: Resolving Conflict

1. They constructively resolve conflict by:
2. directly focusing on the issue, not the person
3. helping participants to stay neutral
4. not being devious
5. staying focused on the issues and not the emotion
6. keeping private things private.
7. They anticipate problems, accept responsibility, and seek solutions.
8. They keep things in perspective, handle one thing at a time, and they don't give up.
9. They are willing to compromise and agree on how to stay on track.
10. They are tolerant of others and deal effectively with those whose background or viewpoints are different from their own.

Chapter 14: Creatively Pro-active and Initiative Driven

1. They are creative and blaze new trails.
2. They challenge conventional practices and search for new and more effective solutions.
3. They take the initiative and get things done.
4. They appreciate and adapt to changing needs.
5. They see change as an opportunity and not a problem.
6. They learn from, recover quickly and move on from mistakes or setbacks.

Promise & Guarantee

If you want to know a principle is true, just live it for a while. Try it out. Test it, and you will come to know. You will never go wrong by doing right.

Likewise, if you want to know if what you have read in this book about greatness is good, then put the principles to the test. This book is not perfect; it may not even be written very well. The next edition will be better. I will just add that when you receive these things, I challenge you to do something about it. Apply these principles in all aspects of your life, and watch for them in the lives of others. I promise you that if you will try with all your heart, might, mind, and strength and with real intent, your "Greatness IQ" and influence will increase dramatically. And, by so doing, you will influence the lives and productivity of many others.

You can be great! You can do it, and you should do it. You need to do it, and the world needs for you to do it. You must decide. You must choose. You will become great and you will know and others too will know. God knows and he is patiently waiting for you. What are you waiting for? Go for it!

Be values driven, mission focused, and passionate about what you do. Be goal oriented and self-motivated. Plan and effectively manage your time and resources. Think strategically; anticipate future moves and adapt through alternative plans and exit strategies. Do the right things rather than just do things right.

Be a leader and mentor who gives vision, direction, and inspiration to others. Be decisive, even at personal risk. Consider how your decisions affect others. Communicate the big picture. Ask questions about expectations. Invite feedback and make it safe for others to disagree. Be the kind of guide to greatness that you hope to have and want to follow.

Never Quit

"Never say the word 'can't',"
- Jennifer Bricker

"Dream big and never give up."
- Nick Vujicic

"Never, never, in nothing great or small, large or petty, never give in except to convictions of honor and good sense. Never yield to force; never yield to the apparently overwhelming might of the enemy . . . Never give up! Never! Never! Never give up!"
- Winston Churchill

In J.R.R. Tolkien's, *The Two Towers*, many are fighting to save the world from great evil. The hero, Frodo, is about to give up in despair when his loyal friend, Sam-wise Gamgee, encourages him:

Frodo: "I can't do this, Sam."

Sam: "I know. It's all wrong. By rights we shouldn't even be here. But we are. It's like in the great stories, Mr. Frodo, the ones that really mattered. Full of darkness and danger, they were. And sometimes you didn't want to know the end. Because how could the end be happy? How could the world go back to the way it was when so much bad had happened?

But in the end, it's only a passing thing, this shadow. Even darkness must pass. A new day will come. And when the sun shines, it will shine out the clearer. Those were the stories that stayed with you. That meant something, even if you were too small to understand why. But I think, Mr. Frodo, I do understand. I know now. Told in those stories, they had lots of chances of turning back, only they didn't. They kept going, because they were holding on to something."

Frodo: "What are we holding onto, Sam?"

Sam: "That there's some good in this world, Mr. Frodo . . . and it's worth fighting for."

About the Author

The author, Dale Christensen, received an MBA from Boston College in 1975 and has had valuable experience in several industries throughout his professional career. He has authored several books, including:

The Shopping Center Acquisition Handbook (1984)
Turning the Hearts (Vol. 1-4, 1983-8)
Thoughts in Verse (1982, 2001, 2005, & 2014)
Entrepreneur's Guide: The Ultimate Business & Learning Experience (2001)
10 Secrets to Speaking English (2001)
A Disciple's Journey (2014)
Patriot's Path (2014)
Dark Horse Candidate (2014).

Dale has also written numerous business-related newspaper articles and is a popular public speaker. He wants to make a difference in people's lives so they will make a difference in the world. He wants to motivate others to apply what they have learned in order to make the world a better place. He wants to be a great teacher and teach others to be the same.

Bibliography

This book makes no attempt to systematically document or identify original sources. Some of the sources quoted, and additional reading sources, include, but are not limited to:

Alien Encounters in the Business World: An Entrepreneur's Guide to Eliminating Failure by Charles K. Stillman and Leonard M. Stillman, Jr. MBA, ParaDynamixX Corp., 1996

As a Man Thinketh by James Allen, Fleming H. Revell Company

Born to Win by Lewis Timberlake and Marietta Reed, Tyndale House Publishing, Inc. 1986

Get Better Or Get Beaten! by Jack Welch and Robert Slater, Richard D. Irwin, Inc. 1994

Management Communications: Principles and Practice by Michael E. Hattersley and Linda McJannet, McGraw-Hill Companies, 1997

Psycho-Cybernetics by Maxwell Maltz, M.D., F.I.C.S, Wilshire Book Company, 1960

Raving Fans by Ken Blanchard and Sheldon Bowles, Blanchard Family Partnership and Ode to Joy Limited, 1993

See You at the Top by Zig Zigler, The Zig Ziglar Corporation, 1975

Systems Analysis in Organizational Behavior by John A. Seiler, Harvard College 1967

The 7 Habits of Highly Effective People by Stephen R. Covey, Simon & Schuster Inc. 1989

The 10 Natural Laws of Successful Time and Life Management by Hyrum W. Smith, Warner Books Inc., 1994

The Future Executive by Harlan Cleveland, Harper & Row, Publishers, 1972

The Leadership Challenge by James M. Kouzes and Barry Z. Posner, Jossey-Bass Inc., Publishers, 1987

The Magic of Thinking Big by David J. Schwartz, Prentice-Hall Inc., 1965

The Richest Man in Babylon by George S. Clason, Hawthorn Books, Inc. 1955

The Time Trap by R. Alec Mackenzie, McGraw-Hill Book Company, 1975

Winning the Negotiations by Henry H. Calero, Hawthorn Books, Inc.